The Prosperity Princess
P.O. Box 707
New Glarus, WI 53574

www.get-a-real-job-online-com

# GET A REAL JOB ONLINE

☐ Work anytime from anywhere
☐ Cut the cost of commute
☐ Jobs leading to career or just extra income

Written and compiled by AnnaMaria Bliven
"The Prosperity Princess"

©Copyright 2013

## TABLE OF CONTENTS

Customer Care Rep ---5
Data Entry --- 29
Editing/Writing ---40
Finance/Accounting/Bookkeeping --64
Insurance ---67
Media and Arts --- 77
Medical Transcription --- 80
Nurses --- 87
Medical Coding --- 93
Medical Call Center --- 95
Physicians --- 98
Jurors --- 102
Education -- 104
Transcription --- not medical --114
    Language translation
Bi-Lingual call center ---120
Bi-Lingual work from home -- 125
Search Evaluation ---133
Micro Tasking ---135
User testing – 139
Computer Technology and IT--141
Social Media --143
Jobs for teens/college students --144
Directions for getting a PayPal Account ---147
Wrap up and Disclaimer ---150

All rights reserved. No part of this publication can be reproduced or transmitted in any form by any means, electronic or mechanical without the expressed permission of the author/compiler.

## Do You Have What It Takes?

Working online is a reality. I know you think "it's just a scam" and that's because according to About.com, there are 42 scams to every 1 real, legitimate job. Yet, since 2002, I have been working legitimate online jobs as a Mystery Shopper, Travel Consultant, College Instructor, Customer Service Representative, and Faculty Evaluator.

It takes a commitment to make it happen. This goes beyond the thought of a "good idea." It takes a commitment to find the work, apply for the work and do the work with excellence.
Do you have what it takes?

The jobs that can lead to careers require time, commitment and dedication to learning the skills needed to do the job tasks and progress in the company. There are some jobs that require you to pass a qualification test. There are also other jobs that can be acquired after you go through short training classes then take and pass a test. Usually after passing the test you can begin work immediately and get paid instantly.

The following are needed to work online jobs:

1. Computer with internet connection
2. Internet DSL works best
3. Phone with a land line (especially for some call center online jobs)
4. Access to a fax machine, scanner (to send application and application materials (i.e. social security card, driver's license, certification, etc.)
5. The working location needs to be in an area of no distractions. (Some companies require you be where there is no background noise)
6. Email address
7. Checking account
8. PayPal account
9. Commitment to perform your work tasks with excellence.
10. Determination and diligence (sometimes you need it)


Now that you know what it takes to be in a position get an online job position, let's look at all the companies that hire online workers. They are listed by career types and then by category.

The companies listed have been checked for legitimacy. There is no guarantee that you will get a job, but if you are determined and diligent, you most likely will land a job online.

Please note: All workers are required to submit tax information. U.S.-based workers need to submit a tax ID or Social Security number. Non-U.S. citizens living outside the United States also need to submit an IRS tax form. U.S. citizens living outside the United States may not work for some of the companies.

*Keep in mind that the Micro Task jobs are always available for fast ways to earn money.*

> *If you are disabled there are certain amounts of money you can make that will not affect your Benefits. Consult your SSI and SSDI office for details.*

# CUSTOMER CARE RESRESENTATIVE

**NewCorp** (https://www.newcorp.com/careers/home_based_ccr)

Are you a professional, dynamic individual with basic computer skills and a knack for helping others and looking for a unique opportunity to work from home?
Do you want to work for a company that has been named one of the "Best Places to Work "for two years in a row?
If the answer is yes—we want to talk to you!

NEW is hiring Home-Based Customer Care Representatives (CCRs) to take inbound customer service and support calls. As a Home-Based CCR, you help customers from the comforts of your home—answering their questions, troubleshooting problems with their product and arranging service or replacement as needed. It's a fulfilling job that gives you a variety of schedules, hourly pay and the opportunity to work from home.

Be Part of Our Virtual Team NEW's Home-Based CCRs span across the country. Through a variety of technologies and a supportive management team, we bring together our diverse group of employees to create a "virtual" team environment similar to our brick and mortar sites. We have virtual chat rooms that allow CCRs to access support, 24/7, should they need assistance. It provides a forum for supervisors and CCRs to communicate about issues and training opportunities.

**News Assurion**
(https://newsasurion.taleo.net/careersection/new_wah_2013_fulltime/jobd etail.ftl?job=1300060&lang=en&portal=54140202819)

*NEW* is hiring Home-Based Customer Care Representatives (CCRs) to take inbound customer service and support calls. As a Home-Based CCR, you help customers from the comforts of your home—answering their questions, troubleshooting problems with their product and arranging service or replacement as needed. It's a fulfilling job that gives you a variety of schedules, hourly pay and the opportunity to work from home.

**Newton Group**
(https://www.newtonelitesalesassociates.com/~newto7/employment.php?pos=1)

The Elite Sales Associate (ESA)
We only hire experienced professionals who have a proven track record of elite professionalism. Because our model is virtual, we can hire from anywhere in the country. Therefore, we only bring on associates that truly

represent the level of professionalism that our clients have grown to expect. As a matter of fact, our clients turn to us because our associates act as an extension of their own sales force.

The Main Objective
As an associate, you will represent our clients to initiate and develop relationships with their potential business prospects. During this process, you will manage the process of collecting valuable market data, understanding the needs of potential prospects, flagging warm leads, and setting appointments. Our software is designed to help you efficiently manage this process, so you can spend less time typing and more time carrying on high quality conversations with the right people. Although our clients request that our associates mention certain key points over the phone, we leave our associates with the autonomy to carry on the conversation. We understand that the ability to have high level conversations is a talent; therefore, we specifically seek out professionals who have displayed these talents through previous work experiences and who can display these talents through the interview process. We are willing to pay more than our competitors because we realize that those individuals with the greatest training and skills get the best results.

The Approval
Because our organization is growing very rapidly, we are always interviewing. Your objective through the interview process is to become an approved Elite Sales Associate. This means that you will be considered for all future campaigns unless your performance proves otherwise.

The Expectations
Must display core values (see mission statement)
Experience in telemarketing, customer service, lead generation, and appointment setting
High level of professionalism
Confidence on the phone with a strong phone presence
Initially work 4 hours per day (Approximately 150 dials)
Reliability and consistency
Discipline to work from home
Able to lead a conversation to extract the desired information
Effective and concise note-taking ability
Ability to type at least 40 WPM
Results that meet client expectations
Positive attitude
Experience using CRM software
Fully-equipped home office with no distractions (more details to follow)

Our Support
We arm our associates with the tools they need to successfully complete each campaign. We work with our associates on a regular basis to help them get the most out of their interactions with these business contacts. Also, we are extremely responsive and strive to keep a healthy and knowledgeable relationship with all of our associates.

Our CRM Software
We developed our own web-based CRM software that manages the process of initiating and developing relationships. As an associate, all you have to do is log in from your home computer to use it. This allows you to spend a very large percentage of your time having high quality conversations with the right people. Prior to working on your first campaign, you will be trained to use the software. The software was designed to be intuitive and easy-to-use. The software also has help screens to answer any questions that you might have. Our system also keeps track of the amount of hours worked, so you know exactly how long you worked, what the results were, and what you can expect to be paid.

Hours
Typically, our associates work four hours a day, Monday thru Friday, and optionally Saturday. For Business to Consumer campaigns, the hours are typically 4:00pm - 9:00pm, and for Business to Business campaigns, 10:00am - 4:45pm, all within the respective time zones. We do require a minimum of 20 hours per associate.

Reliability
We track the number of hours our associates work compared to the number of hours that they commit to working. If our associates fall below a predetermined level, then the relationship can be severely jeopardized or severed. We prefer associates who have a proven track record of working consistently and reliably from their home office. We look for sales associates who are comfortable working at their own residence, and do not see this opportunity as a "work at home, work whenever" situation. We are very understanding of occasional changes in one's schedule. However, all that we ask is that one works 4 solid hours each of the days they are scheduled to work.

"Work-at-Home" Requirements
Comfortable, quiet home office with no distractions
Capable computer system and printer
Reliable high-speed internet (cable or DSL required)
Phone purchased through TNG
Phone headset

Computer System Requirements
Computer: Intel or AMD Processor of 1.8Ghz or faster, with 512MB or more RAM
Operating System: Windows XP SP2 or higher; Mac OS X v10.5 or higher; Linux v2.6 or higher
Firewall installed & operating
Current anti-virus protection & spyware/malware detection
Router (minimum of 4 ports); Recommended: D-Link DIR-655

Internet Requirements
Reliable high-speed Internet (No satellite, wireless ISP, or dial-up)
Wireless connection within your home is acceptable, as long as your DSL or Cable connection is hard wired
Web Browser: Internet Explorer 7 or higher; Mozilla Firefox 3.5 or higher; Google Chrome 6+

Contact Us
If you are interested in completing the necessary steps in becoming an Elite Sales Associate, please e-mail your resume to the human resources manager at jobs@newtonesa.com and request the Agent Qualifications - Basic Requirements document. All applicants must submit a resume before they will be considered for an interview.

* Note: Applicants must reside in and be a citizen of the United States

**Pierce Eislen**
(http://www.pi-ei.com/Careers.aspx)

Pierce-Eislen, a Scottsdale-based national real estate research firm has need for a research associate.

Desired personal characteristics include:

Attention to detail
College graduate
Experience in an office environment
Real Estate document experience
Advanced knowledge of PC Windows, Word, Excel, Access, and Internet skills.

Please email your resume, and entry level salary requirement, to Robin Nathanson: Robin.Nathanson@Yardi.com or fax: (480) 663-6269

**Pleio Good Start**
(http://www.goodstartu.info/)

We are looking for caring, motivated individuals who want to assist others with getting into a good routine with their medication. If you are a self-sufficient, self-starter with a home office, a dedicated phone line, and have a desire to help people, apply now!


**Cruise.com**
(http://www.cruise.com/cruise-information/employment.asp?skin=001)

To be considered, email your resume to jobs@cruise.com indicating your job objective. If you are applying for one of our home-based career opportunities, please detail your recent cruise industry customer service or cruise sales experience in your email or on your resume. Without this information, consideration for an interview will not be given.

CURRENT HOME-BASED JOB OPPORTUNITIES (MULTI-STATE)
Cruise.com is now recruiting home-based cruise sales and customer service specialists for our January 2014 training classes. Each class will be held from Monday through Friday, 10 a.m. to 7 p.m. (EST), for three consecutive weeks. Training is web-based and accessed from your home office computer/internet provider (no travel required). Only candidates whose initial resumes or job applications reflect prior cruise industry experience will be considered. Phone interviews will be scheduled based on an analysis of the candidates' qualifications for the position. Training is paid, and all positions offer a base salary plus commission or incentive plan and an attractive employee benefits package including eligibility for travel agent benefits through IATAN membership.

*Cruise Sales Agents* (Home-Based) - Requires at least 2 years of recent cruise sales work experience, preferably in a call center environment selling all of the major cruise lines. Language fluency in English/Spanish or English/French or English/Russian is required for some openings. Purpose: To sell cruise vacations, insurance, and other product options to potential customers through inbound/outbound telephone calls/e-mail leads. To close the sale of a cruise booking, up selling cruise packages to maximize revenue. To meet or exceed minimum monthly sales productivity goals there are incentives. Base pay plus commission plan.

*Online Support Agents* (Home-Based) - Requires at least 1 year of recent cruise sales experience, preferably in a call center environment selling all of the major cruise lines. Purpose: To answer incoming calls from customers for the purposes of resolving problems, providing information, converting inquiries into invoices, selling travel insurance and answering questions while providing high level service to our customers. To meet or exceed minimum monthly productivity goals there are incentives. Base pay plus incentive plan.

*Customer Service Agent* (Home-Based) - Requires at least 1 year of recent cruise industry call center experience in either sales or customer service. Related cruise industry experience is required. Purpose: To answer incoming calls from customers for the purposes of resolving problems, providing information, and answering questions while providing high level service to our customers. Base pay plus incentive plan.

**Sykes** (formerly Alpine Express) (https://jobs.alpineaccess.com/)

SYKES Home Powered by Alpine Access is a leader in the virtual contact center industry, specializing in SaaS-based talent management, cloud-based security and consulting services. With a workforce of 6,700 customer care professionals dispersed throughout the U.S. and Canada, this home-based customer contact solution supports more than 30 brands across 50 programs. Our industry-leading clients include Fortune 1000 companies in retail, financial services, telecommunications, healthcare, technology, travel and hospitality, media and entertainment. But whatever the industry, we are dedicated to working side-by-side with each of our clients to create customized, versatile solutions that generate high value for their business.

Our Employees are delivering consistent quality and superior performance, our experienced customer care professionals work as expert extensions of our clients' brands. Comprised of people from diverse demographics – including those with impaired mobility, retirees, parents, adult students, veterans and military spouse – the success of SYKES Home is a direct result of the "passion to serve" and positive attitude of all our employees.

**Talk2Rep** (http://www.talk2rep.com/news18.htm)

Talk2Rep Call Centers are currently hiring over 500 representatives for opportunities in both their Florida facilities and nationally for work at home positions. Positions include customer service, telemarketing, and on-line chat support for Talk2Rep's healthcare, telecommunications and utility clients.

"We are both fortunate and pleased to be afforded the opportunity to contribute to both the Florida and national economy by hiring only US citizens to work at home and in our call centers. We find that we can compete effectively against offshore companies by offering superior skills and services with US based employees," said Talk2Rep CEO Jim Ryan.

Talk2Rep invests heavily in recruiting and "highest quality call center agent" modeling to target and select the best US based employees possible. That's followed up with extensive, client specific training and education that result in superior service for our clients. "Our goal is to service our clients customers so that we get it right the first time and we strive to reduce repetitive calls to solve a problem or close a sale. Initial job requirements for all positions include basic computer skills, good typing and internet skills along with a great attitude and a focus on assisting people. Talk2Rep's Florida call center based employees also require strong selling skills while work at home agents must have access to a high speed internet connection. All agents must pass various assessment tests and background checks.


**Intrep**
(http://www.flexjobs.com/jobs/telecommuting-jobs-at-intrep)

Intrep is a telesales company based out of Franklin Park, New Jersey that has been providing superior inside sales support since 1999. Intrep is owned by its founders, Mark Winwood and Dan Greenberg who have spent a combined 55 years working in sales, marketing and operations management in a variety of business-to-business industries. Since the majority of their sales associates work from home, Intrep puts candidates through a very in-depth screening process because they hire only the best of the best in sales and marketing professionals. However, Intrep rewards all its home based agents with higher than average wages, benefits, and opportunities for additional training and bonus programs.


**DeRosa Communications** (http://www.derosa.com/callteam.htm)

Appointment setting
Lead generation and qualifying
Sales pipeline management

Although there are no positions to immediately fill, the nature of the business is dynamic and needs do frequently surface. We also get inquiries from prospective clients with business models that are not a fit for us and we would be happy to put you in touch with them with both of your permissions. We try our best to match specific requirements with the appropriate skill and experience sets. To that end, there is a form to complete to tell about your special attributes. The information provided is kept private and not shared with anyone or any entity without your written permission.

**Adecco**
(http://www/adeccousa.com/call-center-and-customer-service/job-seekers/Pages/types-of-work.aspx)

**http://www.adeccousa.com/call-center-and-customer-service/Pages/PassiveApply.aspx**

Adecco offers you a few different ways to connect with top companies – depending on your schedule and your career needs.

<u>Temporary work</u> is a great way to gain experience in a variety of jobs and get your foot in the door with a variety of companies. If you're someone who values flexibility, we can help you find work on your schedule — on an as-needed, day-to-day basis, or on an indefinite contract. Plus, as an Adecco call center and customer service temporary associate, you get access to our comprehensive group medical plan, 401(k), skills training, and more.

<u>Temporary-to-permanent employment</u>: If you think you're ready for a full-time position, but want to test the waters a little first, a temporary-to-permanent arrangement gives you the best of both worlds. You'll get a feel for what it's like to work for certain employers (while earning a paycheck) and decide if you want to sign on — or move on — when the time comes.

<u>Permanent employment</u>: Ready to make a long-term commitment? We've been doing this for a while, so we have lots of connections with top employers — and we know which ones are looking to fill permanent positions. Improving your career is our full-time job. Let us introduce you to your next career opportunity.

**Arise** (http://www.arise.com/company/join-our-team/corporate-positions)

Arise Virtual Solutions is a well known virtual call center company that is often mentioned in the media as a legit work-at-home opportunity. Arise agents absorb business costs--in the form of training and other ongoing fees. For the agent, investing in this cost upfront makes Arise a riskier business proposition.

**ACD Direct** (http://www.acddirect.com/becomeanagent.cfm)

ACD Direct seeks experienced customer service professionals to process calls in our virtual call center! Turn your experience into $$$ while starting a fun and rewarding opportunity!

You schedule when you want, what times you want and what days you wish to work!

**Accolade Support**
(http://www.accoladesupport.com/openings.html)

We are looking for bright and energetic people to work from home.

Position Title: Call Center Agent
Position Type: Contract - Part Time
Compensation: $7.25 to $9.00 per hour
Start Date: Immediately


Description:
Accolade Support is a rapidly growing division of Tier 3 Support, Inc. We are looking for remote agents to join our team, working from home on an on-call basis. We'll get a schedule of your available hours and when our call volume rises during your available hours, we'll contact you to take calls from your home. This is the ideal position for someone who is around his or her home on a regular basis and is looking to make a little extra money in their spare time.

We're looking for bright, energetic individuals who enjoy speaking with people on the phone, and possess the in-depth understanding and the diverse skills to provide callers with the highest quality of service. Our clients demand the highest service level possible. In turn, we are constantly working to build a team of friendly and efficient support professionals to meet our current clients growing call volumes, as well as the numerous new clients we begin services for each month.


Applicants should possess the following skill set:

Technical skills - A technical skill set with the ability to provide desktop troubleshooting, resolve Internet connectivity issues, and support software applications (with training).

Sales skills - The ability to sell products and services to a wide variety of markets to inbound callers.

Customer service skills - Working with callers who may be frustrated or upset that something hasn't gone as expected. A key component of this is assuring the customer that you will help them, calming them down, and resolving the situation for them when possible. Patience and a genuine desire to assist our customers is a must.

Attention to detail - Callers will regularly relate information including phone numbers, email addresses, product numbers, messages, and details about their particular reason for calling. Accurately relaying this information to our clients is crucial to your success in this position.

To qualify for this position you must have, or obtain the following:

1. A U.S. based home telephone number. (No cell phones or VOIP phones)
2. A corded telephone set with a headset. (No cordless phones)
3. A PC with Windows 98, or 2000, or XP
4. Your PC wired to a cable modem, DSL modem, or broadband connection. (No wireless connections)
5. A quiet environment where you can take calls without being disrupted or callers hearing any noise or sounds in the background


You must meet the following criteria to qualify for this position:

1. You must be geographically located in The United States,
2. You must be able to provide proof of having the legal right to work in the United States.
3. You must be willing to submit to a criminal background check.

To apply for this position please emails your resume in Microsoft Word Format, or Adobe Acrobat PDF format to us at: hr@tier3support.com. No telephone calls please.


**Micah Tek**
(http://www.flexjobs.com/jobs/telecommuting-jobs-at-micahtek_inc.)

MicahTek, Inc. is known globally as a full turn-key service center that provides a broad spectrum of information management and distribution services. Call Center, Live Agents, Interactive Voice Recognition, Website Design and Development, Registration and Events, Database Management and Hosting, and Product Fulfillment and Warehousing. The company is experiencing a period of rapid growth and therefore has multiple opportunities to work from home as a home based contract customer service agents. These positions are full time, with some degree of flexibility available. Training is provided to qualified candidates who are then allowed to work from the comfort of their home as virtual professionals. To find out more about the telecommuting opportunities that MicahTek can offer you, be sure to check out the links here on Flex jobs for great jobs.


**NTI**
(http://www.nticentral.org/work-at-home-jobs-disabled.shtm)

NTI provides job opportunities for Americans with disabilities that require home-based work.

Who should apply?
If you're an American who is disabled and would like to work from home, you may qualify for an online job in customer service, technical support, medical transcription, quality control, or many other types of work.

Legitimate at-home jobs
NTI, a nonprofit organization, has worked for over 15 years with employers, Social Security Disability Insurance, and with vocational rehabilitation services that work with disabled individuals. We match people like you with legitimate work-at-home opportunities suited to your situation and requirements.

Apply now
New job openings are arriving all the time. Apply now to be a part of NTI's database of pre-screened, pre-qualified applicants. We'll follow up to identify what jobs you're interested in and try to match you with a suitable work-at-home opportunity.


**EBI** (Employee Background Investigations) **Solutions**
(https://ebiinc.ercdataplus.com/jobseeker/main_intro.php?ERCSESSID=q8fbf5vbnf4v6kuh90bgeq6ql4)

The success of EBI comes deep within the passion and the soul of our staff and our partners. The only way that we will continually be viewed as a leader in the eyes of our industry is through the vision and commitment of our people and partners. We provide opportunities for individuals to develop their skills, further their careers and to embrace our mutual goal as the leading brand of choice in the screening industry. Our company offers a wide range of career opportunities, including *Verification and Processing Specialists, Customer Care and Strategic Account Managers*, among many others.

EBI is always on the lookout for talented individuals. If you are interested in joining our team, please login and complete and application today!

**Prospect Image**
(http://www.prospectimage.com/careers.php)

*Production Assistant Contractor*

We are looking for someone who is a quick learner. Position requires 2-4 hours per day depending on account. Training will be provided. Independent Contractor will be paid $10 per hour plus bonuses. Hourly rate will increase with experience.

Duties Include:

Cold Calling Businesses
Appointment Setting
Data Entry
Database Management
Sending Faxes and/or Mailings
Filling out Daily Worksheet

Requirements:

Separate business phone line
Basic computer skills
Microsoft Excel
2-4 hours per day of uninterrupted quiet time
Excellent organization skills
Good articulation and pleasant phone voice
DBA License (if necessary in your county)
To apply, please send resume to jobs@prospectimage.com

**Just Answer**
(http://www.justanswer.com/expert/credential/become_an_expert.aspx)
We invite you to join a community of professionals who answer questions on JustAnswer and Pearl.com. You will answer questions on your own time, and get paid by our rapidly growing customer base of more than 20 million people and counting.
To join the community of professionals, you will need to:
   Complete an online application and online profile
   Take a short subject matter test
   Verify your credentials

**Kelly Services**
(http://www.kellyservices.us/US/Careers/KellyConnect/Kelly-At-Home/#.UrymBdJDvHQ)

Stable company. Steady work. As a highly regarded and reputable employer with more than 60 years of experience employing people like you, we offer professional and credible work at home opportunities. We're committed to providing our employees with the resources necessary to work at home successfully, including paid training and a dedicated support staff that's only a phone call away. There are no start-up fees, and you'll be paid for the hours you work, not just your call time.

Our work at home hiring process is simple and convenient! Most steps are automated and can be completed in the comfort of your own home.
1. Complete our online prequalification questions.
The online prequalification is a brief questionnaire that asks basic questions to ensure you have the critical skills and appropriate work environment necessary for working at home.
2. Participate in a telephone interview with a Kelly recruiter.
A Kelly recruiter will assess your qualifications to make certain you possess the minimum requirements and ensure you will be placed on an assignment that best suits your skills, abilities, and desires.
3. Complete online testing.
Our online testing will assess your technical contact center skills to help determine the types of positions for which you are best suited.
4. Complete online on boarding.
From the convenience of your own home, you will access our innovative on boarding application and submit all necessary hiring information.
5. Visit your local Kelly branch to complete the necessary I-9 paperwork.
You are required to complete your I-9 documents in the presence of a Kelly staff member.
6. The Kelly Services team will work with you to identify positions that match your qualifications and provide support and guidance while you are working.

**Working Solutions** (www.workingsolutions.com/)
Industry:
Business Process Outsourcing (BPO) that provides inbound technical support, sales and customer service as well as data entry and editing services.

Company Description:
Based in Plano, TX, Working Solutions bills itself as "the first company to utilize an entire workforce of home-based customer sales and service agents." Founded in 1996, the company utilizes independent contractor

virtual call center agents, which it calls "Agents On Demand," to services clients' call center needs. Additionally it also hires contractors for data entry work.

Qualifications:
Applicants must be 18 years old. Working Solutions "looks for skilled, educated, and motivated people" to fill its ranks. Agents are required to provide their own computer equipment (with Windows Vista or higher) and Internet service (DSL or cable).

Types of Work-at-Home Positions:
Working Solutions hires independent contractors to work on a project basis in home call centers and on data entry.
Virtual call center agents handle inbound and outbound customer service, sales, market research and/or technical support. These positions could include enrollments, retail sales, reservations, account support and technical assistance on electronics, websites, software and telephony. Agents work with customers over the phone, through online chat and email.
The company also seeks bilingual agents with fluency in Arabic, Bengali, Cantonese, Creole, Filipino, French, French-Canadian, German, Hindi, Italian, Japanese, Korean, Mandarin, Portuguese, Russian, Samoan, Spanish and Vietnamese. Company also hires travel agents with knowledge of Apollo, Amadeus, Galileo, Sabre or WorldSpan and corporate booking experience.

Pay and Benefits:
Because Working Solutions hires independent contractors there is no guarantee of minimum wage or any number of hours per week. However, the position is likely a part-time call center job. The company says its projects, which all compensate differently, pay anywhere from $7.50 to $30 an hour. However, they may not necessarily calculate pay on an hourly rate. Agents invoice Working Solutions, based on their projects' pay instructions, and are paid every two weeks.
Again because it hires independent contractors, the company does not offer benefits of any kind. Agents are able to choose their own hours online. However, the availability of hours can vary making it difficult to earn a full-time living at Working Solutions. Despite their status as independent contractors, agents aren't charged any fees by the company.

Geographic Restrictions:
The company hires Agents OnDemand in all U.S. states and from across the world. However the number of projects, particularly call center jobs, for residents outside the U.S. is more limited.

Applying to Working Solutions:
Submit an application online through the company's website. You may paste a resume into the comments field of the application. At the end of the online application, you will be asked to answer a few questions in part one of an assessment. Multiple choice and written-answer questions will test your knowledge of customer service as well as assess your grammar and writing skills.

After submitting this, you will be able to complete the second part of the assessment. For this you will call in and record answers regarding customer service scenarios. After this your application will be evaluated and you will be notified if your application will be placed in the "pending pool," meaning that you will be considered for opportunities that match your qualifications. If there is a match you will be contacted by email. It can take several weeks to months to be matched with the first project.

**Teletech** (http://www.teletechjobs.com/athome-en-US/search-home-jobs/)
Customer service
TeleTech offers a world of opportunities—literally. With service delivery centers in 17 countries worldwide, TeleTech provides a great opportunity for you to gain valuable experience working with diverse clients, customers, and cultures every day. In fact, our associates interact daily with more than 3.5 million customers in nearly 30 different languages around the world via phone, Internet, email, and other media.

**iTelesource**
(http://www.itelesource.com/careers/apply/)
Lead generation
Lead qualification
Sales outsourcing

iTelesource is looking for experienced professionals.

iTelesource is growing fast, and with this success comes the challenge of finding exceptional people with a passion for sales lead generation. iTelesource offers great perks such as the ability to work from home, flexible schedules, and excellent pay. If you are an outgoing professional with a take charge attitude please review the following positions.

*Business Development Representative:* Are you a sales professional with a passion for cold calling? Do you wish to spend more time at home and less on the road? iTelesource offers a great alternative to the road weary sales professional.

As a Business Development Representative for iTelesource you will make outbound calls from your home office pitching our client's solutions to their targeted accounts. You must be able to craft a solution from research and dialogue that generates interest in our clients. You will log all time and activities via CRM as well as participate in weekly client calls. You must display the utmost of professionalism in all activities representing iTelesource and our clients. Training will be provided on all client engagements.

Requirements: (Must Meet ALL)

- Home office with unlimited long distance plan
- Ability to work 20+ hours per week during business hours
- 5-10 years sales experience in a Complex Sales environment
- Experience calling on VP and C level
- Knowledge of various technologies and business industries a plus
- Experience in multiple CRMs


**KGB** (http://kgb.com/about)

Customer care business operates in the U.S. and Europe and has over ten years of experience in providing call center support for many leading customer service and sales-oriented organizations across a variety of industry groups, including telecommunications, cable, utilities, government, and health care.
In 2010, kgb harnessed its database of hyper-local directory assistance information to launch *www.kgbdeals.com*, a deal site that brings its members daily discounts on popular products and services; By March 2011, kgbdeals was offering deals in more than 100 cities globally and had become the third largest daily deal business in the world. Also in 2010 in the U.S. and Europe, KGB launched *www.kgbpeople.com*, a people search engine that enables consumers to monitor their profile on the Web, set alerts, and manage their reputation online. Last year kgb served more than a hundred million consumers globally.

**Blooms Today**
(http://www.flexjobs.com/jobs/telecommuting-jobs-at-blooms_today\)

Blooms Today is a flower and gift company that offers same-day delivery by a florist located in the same community as each customer. In order to expand its business worldwide, Blooms Today partners with 1-800Flowers, FTD, and Teleflora, and it is a member of the Society of American Florists. Though headquartered in Haymarket, Virginia, Blooms Today reaches worldwide and has a strong customer service focus with a satisfaction guarantee. Blooms Today offers a wide array of floral arrangements and gifts for all major holidays, and for a variety of life's moments, with gifts including gourmet baskets and sweets. As an employer, Blooms Today often seeks full-time and part-time talent, and hires additional talent around major flower-related holidays like Mother's Day.

**Enterprise Car Rental**
(http://careers.enterprise.com/careers/work-from-home-jobs)

By being hired into one of our Work from Home jobs at Enterprise Holdings, you'll be a key member of the Enterprise Holdings team. Professionals in Work from Home careers come from a variety of backgrounds, bringing an assortment of knowledge and skills to every area of our business. Please click on your desired Work from Home job below to learn more about the exact qualifications.
A job in Work from Home at Enterprise Holdings may be waiting for you!

**Grind stone**
(http://www.flexjobs.com/jobs/telecommuting-jobs-at-grindstone)

Requirements - We are seeking Talented "Outbound" Telemarkers only
3 years of successful Business to Business Appointment Setting or Direct Sales Experience speaking with Business Owners, CEO's, Presidents and decision makers' professional upbeat sounding telephone voice.
A desire to interact with prospective customers with consultative selling approach ability to take direction and follow through high-Speed Internet access.

AOL Instant Messenger
Microsoft Outlook
Anti-virus protection program
Unlimited Long Distance calling plan
Computer/Internet experience and skills

Recruiting and retaining the best talent is one of the keys to Grindstone's success. Our highest priority is to find and keep the best people, no matter where they may be!

We are always looking for talented professionals to join our team. Work from your remote office, If you have a great phone voice, are organized and experienced in the services we provide our clients, then we want to talk to you. The majority of our clients need assistance in the Technology and Business Services sector, although we are successful with clients in other industries as well
Our clients demand that we hire the best. Those who pass our thorough screening process will have the opportunity to flourish with a growing company. We are on the cutting edge of a new trend, and we believe in promoting from within.

Not afraid to pick up the phone? Ready to join a fantastic company? This work at home career maybe just the thing for you!

**Intelichek**
(http://intelichek.simplicant.com/job/detail/10859)

InteliChek is a market research company specializing in collecting data to analyze what is happening in different markets and different industries. We do this by calling businesses across the North America and gathering information about the products and services they offer and the price of those products and services. Some of the data we have gathered include the cost of an oil change, the price of a specific tire, warranty information, hours of operation, etc.

We are always looking for great people that want to work on their terms and their schedule, who are reliable and have good communication skills.

**Maritz Researchers**
(http://www.maritzresearch.com/about/careers-survey-center-opportunities.aspx)

We are looking for professional, loyal, self motivated employees to conduct customer satisfaction surveys. These part time positions offer quality employment, flexible scheduling, and an opportunity to learn about market research.

This position conducts market research/customer satisfaction surveys. Absolutely no sales or solicitation involved.

Basic Job Requirements:

Friendly Personality
Proficient in general computer usage
Ability to read verbatim and follow instructions.

Virtual Call Center – Work from Home
Requirements include: a good infrastructure to include a landline, computer and good internet provider, and a quiet work environment.

**My Favorite Mouse**
(http://www.myfavoritemouse.com/join.html)

Join Our Team:
As an " EARMARKED "Authorized Disney Vacation Planning Company, GalaxSea Cruises and Tours is seeking a very elite group of passionate Disney fans to sell Disney Destination vacations.
If you are the kind of magical person who :
Is answering questions now , for family and friends , to help them plan their Disney Destination vacations
Has an extended knowledge of Disney Theme Parks and Resort Hotels Schedules character dining, behind the scenes tours , parade times , fireworks viewing times and more . . . . .
Has personal Disney travel experiences that you enjoy sharing with contacts so you have become the " GO TO PERSON " for magical answers ... always thinks of how much fun it would be to sell Disney vacations and make others " Dreams Come True "
Then . . . you may have the qualities we are searching for to become part of our Authorized Disney Vacation Planning Sales Team !
To be considered for the position, please email your resume and list of Disney Travel experiences to: info@myfavoritemouse.com


**NCO Group** (http://www.ncogroup.com/careers/)
NCO is an industry leader in providing clients with successful business process outsourcing (BPO) solutions. Our outstanding portfolio includes accounts receivable management, customer management services, and back office services for a diversified customer base.

NCO operates a global network of over 100 operations centers running on a centralized data platform with the flexibility to respond to a rapidly changing marketplace, and to scale operations to meet client specifications. Our International presence is across the United States, Canada, India, United Kingdom, Philippines, Antigua, Panama, Australia, Mexico, Guatemala and Uruguay.

NCO is an equal opportunity affirmative action employer, and a drug-free workplace committed to a diverse workforce. NCO is a customer driven company dedicated to meeting the client's needs. NCO is continually searching for career-minded professionals who are looking for challenging and rewarding career opportunities in a fast-paced environment.

NCO values and supports all U.S. military personnel, veterans, and disabled veterans who have provided dedicated service to keep our country free and maintain our civil liberties. NCO is committed to supporting the employment of these veterans, as we value the commitment, work ethic and experience that they bring to the job market. NCO invites you to explore available career opportunities and encourages all qualified persons to apply through our online process. Should you qualify and are selected as the most suitable candidate for the position, we would be honored to have you become part of the NCO team.

**Needle.com**
(https://pincushion.needle.com/needlers/welcome/)

Chat online for clients such as Coach, Overstock,etc …
Needle has partnered with several internet retailers to provide shoppers with live product expertise from fans like you who know and use their products.

If selected, you will:
Chat online with customers and help them find the right products
Set your own schedule, work as a 1099 contractor
Compensated with cash, plus earn points to redeem for cool products.

**Neiman Markus**
(http://www.neimanmarcuscareers.com/wfh/index.shtml)

The Neiman Marcus Direct Work From Home (WFH) program offers you a unique opportunity to provide exceptional customer service from the comfort of your own home to our distinguished web and catalog customers. With the advancement of technology, you will enjoy this job and still have time to do the things that are important to you. Every day our Work From Home Associates transform their home into a virtual customer support center. Through phone calls, live chats and email, associates manage all our customers' contacts with diligence and an unwavering commitment to excellence. The Neiman Marcus Direct Marketing segment conducts both print catalog and online operations under the Neiman Marcus, Horchow and Bergdorf Goodman brands.

Our Work From Home program will allow you to:

Work without a dress code
Cut down on transportation costs and commute time (*)
Have flexibility with personal and family priorities

At Neiman Marcus Direct, our employees are the "Cornerstone" of our business. We care about your growth and are committed to providing you with the necessary tools to be successful. You will attend a three-week-long training which includes time allotted for on-the-job practice, after which you will join "Cornerstone," our production mentoring program. For two additional weeks you will be guided by a group of high performers to ensure you have a successful transition after you have graduated from training.

As an employee of Neiman Marcus Direct, you will join a company that has been operating since 1907. We are a modern company that is still very much based on the principles of our founders. That is why we remain dedicated to exceptional customer service and superior merchandising. If you are looking for a home-based career opportunity, then consider Neiman Marcus Direct.

**OPK Telemarketing**
(http://www.opktelemarketing.com/jobs.html)

You can work from your home office as an independent contractor for OPK— join OPK Telemarketing Services' team of elite business professionals. OPK is seeking callers who already have several years of sales and/or telemarketing experience. Please tell us more about yourself by submitting a resume and cover letter.

Please submit your resume and cover letter to:

OPK Telemarketing Services
PO Box 3245
Greenwood Village, CO 80155

**Smart Office Solutions**
(http://www.flexjobs.com/jobs/telecommuting-jobs-at-smart_office_solutions_inc.)

Smart Office Solutions is a full range office services company based in Orlando, FL. They provide services like conference calling, web conferences, fax and voice mail on demand, virtual office administrative support and sales support. The company is experiencing a period of rapid growth and therefore has multiple opportunities to work from home as a customer service representative. These positions are full time, with some degree of flexibility available and excellent hourly pay and benefits. Training is provided to qualified candidates who are then allowed to work from the comfort of their home as virtual professionals. To find out more about the telecommuting opportunities that Smart Office Solutions can offer you, be sure to check out the links here on Flex jobs for great jobs with this expanding company.

**Starwood Hotels**
*Starwood Hotels Reservation at home agent*
(http://www.flexjobs.com/jobs/telecommuting-jobs-at-starwood_hotels_&_resorts)

Founded in 1969 and one of the foremost hotel and leisure corporations in the world, Starwood Hotels & Resorts employs nearly 145,000 employees in 942 properties across 100 countries. Headquartered in White Plains, New York, the distinguished list of international hotels owned and managed by Starwood Hotels includes St. Regis, Sheraton®, Westin, Le Méridien, Four Points. Starwood Vacation Ownership, Inc., a subsidiary of Starwood Hotels, is also leading provider of luxury timeshare resorts. The notable corporation is dedicated to maintaining its standard of excellence through innovation, continued growth, diversity and empowered employees. Starwood offers employees great benefits and pay, an engaging work environment and recognition for talent and hard work.

Full-time, part-time, telecommuting opportunities are offered.


**U-Haul Customer Service** (http://jobs.uhaul.com/moonlighter.aspx)

Are you interested in becoming a moonlighter? Are you looking for another job to supplement your income? If so, U-Haul is the right place for you! Moonlighters are important and valued members of the U-Haul Team because they help us meet our customers' needs - which are significantly greater on evenings, weekends and holidays - with skilled, talented people who will provide excellent customer service.

Whether you're "regular" job is a full-time or part-time position at another company, being in the military, going to school or being a stay-at-home parent, the flexible schedules available at U-Haul will make it possible for you to join our team. We have a variety of positions available for moonlighters and the flexible schedules we offer provide many options.


**VForce Auto Club Renewals**
(http://www.flexjobs.com/jobs/telecommuting-jobs-at-vforce_auto_club_renewals)

Current job data is reserved for active Flex Jobs members. Please login or register now to access this specific information. However, we have included some of their past telecommuting jobs, to provide you an idea of the types of jobs Vforce Auto Club Renewals has hired for in the past (and which they may be likely to hire for again!).
Seeking friendly people who can build relationships on the phone. Must have a sales background and be able to make cold calls. Telecommute.

**Westat**
(http://www.westat.com/Westat/careers/career_area_desc.cfm)
Career Area Descriptions)

Research
Westat's research staff comprises people with diverse training and experience in statistics, economics, social sciences, education, health sciences, and many other fields that support research programs. We hire subject-matter experts, project directors, study managers, survey designers, research analysts, field operations directors, research assistants, and many other research professionals.

Research - Health Studies
Westat has conducted or supported health research for numerous public and private sector clients. These projects use mail and telephone surveys, in-person interviewing, record abstracting, physical examinations, nutrition assessments, and other methods for descriptive studies. Experimental studies include trials of therapeutic agents and diagnostic tests, as well as clinical and community disease prevention studies. Our involvement ranges from short-term support to long-range planning and design for multiyear, multicenter projects.

Research - Clinical Trials
Westat provides complete contract research organization services for Phase I-IV clinical trials and epidemiologic studies in a variety of therapeutic areas for adult and pediatric populations. From initial evaluation in humans, through controlled clinical trials, to regulatory approval and postmarking surveillance, Westat manages all phases of the clinical development process.

Computer Systems & Applications
Westat's computer systems and applications development capabilities are central to our work. These capabilities begin with our more than 450 systems analysts and programmers working mostly on Windows-based systems in our corporate network environment. They create and maintain a wide variety of Web, database, and other types of sophisticated applications and systems for our diverse research projects.

Administrative
Westat's corporate infrastructure contributes greatly to the success of its contract work. Professionals with experience in a variety of fields, such as accounting and contracts, editorial and word processing, facility operations, graphic arts, human resources, library services, PC and

telecommunications, and security operations, among others, work to support Westat projects and corporate goals.

Survey Processing

Westat employs staff members to perform administrative, data collection, and data processing duties on current Westat research projects. Some assignments require personnel who are bilingual, where English is one of the languages spoken. Survey processing staff positions are paid on an hourly basis. Benefits are based on hours worked and tenure. A high school degree or its equivalent is required. We provide easy access to public transportation with discounted Metro/Ride-On cards and free parking at our offices in Rockville, Maryland.

Telephone Data Collection

Westat employs skilled telephone data collection staffs who administer questionnaires over the telephone. Our studies are typically conducted in English but often require individuals who can also conduct interviews in other languages. Westat has Telephone Research Centers located in three states across the continental United States. Additionally, Westat has telephone data collectors who work from their homes.

Telephone data collection centers are located in the following cities:

Rockville, Maryland
Frederick, Maryland
Gaithersburg, Maryland
Merced, California
Telephone data collectors are paid on an hourly basis.

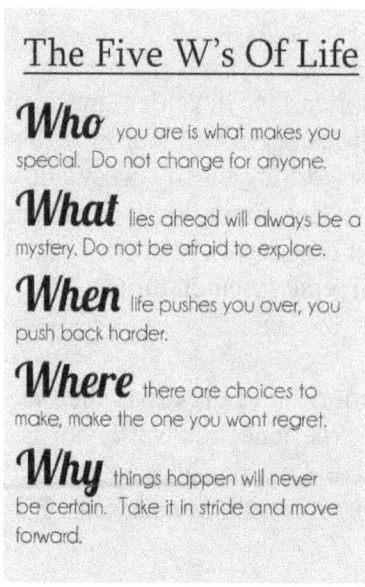

The Five W's Of Life

**Who** you are is what makes you special. Do not change for anyone.

**What** lies ahead will always be a mystery. Do not be afraid to explore.

**When** life pushes you over, you push back harder.

**Where** there are choices to make, make the one you wont regret.

**Why** things happen will never be certain. Take it in stride and move forward.

# DATA ENTRY

**Axion Data Services** (www.axiondata.com)

Pennsylvania-based data outsourcing firm Axion Data Services hires independent contractors to perform data entry for its clients. These jobs are performed off-site and usually from home.

Data entry jobs at this company pay independent contractors on a per-piece basis. The company accepts applications when it has jobs available.

Types of Work-at-Home Opportunities at Axion Data Services: The data entry work that Axion offers is entering data from scanned images. Some of the types of data entry projects that Axion contractors work on are loyalty program applications, contest entries, advertising insertions, customer response cards, student records, product registrations and questionnaires.

Most of its operators work part time, 20-25 hours per week, but the amount of work available may vary. However, when an agent works those hours is usually flexible. Agents log on to Axion's system, review available projects and choose which ones to do.

Qualifications and Requirements:
Basic computer skills, such as installing and removing software, creating new folders, sending email and using the Internet, are absolutely required. Additionally, accurate data entry skills and following instructions are important qualifications. Operators must provide and maintain their own computer—either a Windows PC or Mac system—or a high speed Internet connection. Contractors must have either a telephone answering machine or voice mail. Contractors will have to download some free software and may be required to purchase software.

Successful applicants will have a clean criminal and must sign a confidentiality agreement.

Pay and Benefits: All data entry agents are hired as independent contractors. This means there are no benefits and no guarantee of minimum wage.

Axion Data pays its data entry operators on a per-piece basis, which varies based on the complexity of the project. For example in some projects, the data entered is small, and agents can input 2 to 4 forms per minute at a compensation rate ranging from 4 to 8 cents per form. This works out to a potential range of $4.80 to $19.20 per hour; though, keep in mind that earning the top number is unlikely because faster jobs likely have a lower rate. Other projects require 30 to 60 minutes per document, with compensation ranging from $5-9 per document (potentially $5 to $18 per hour). Agents submit invoices for their work every two weeks and are paid 28 days later.

**Amazon Mechanical Turk** (https://www.mturk.com/mturk/welcome)

One of the earliest and best known *crowd sourcing* marketplaces, Amazon's Mechanical Turk, also called MTurk, and utilizes what it calls the "human intelligence" of an army of independent contractors who complete small online tasks. These online tasks are things that its "requesters," or clients, need real people, not computers, to do. This work-at-home division of Amazon is part of Amazon's Web Services division and is separate from the online retailer's home call center employees.

Types of Work-at-Home Opportunities at Mechanical Turk: Online workers at Mechanical
Turk accepts HITs, or "human intelligence tasks," and is paid small sums for each. Though Amazon is a U.S.-based company, workers (and requesters) come from all over the globe. Because of this global diversity, what HITs pay and what they require can vary greatly. Some jobs might pay 1 or 2 cents but take only minutes to complete and require very little expertise of the worker. Other HITs require workers to gain qualifications before being allowed to work on them. Qualification may be a test but it could also simply be approval or rejection based on your previous work, location, profile, etc. Jobs with qualification presumably pay more. Unlike some other micro job sites, which may offer real-world and online tasks, Mechanical Turk is completely online.

The types of task might include:
Surveys
Blog comments
Transcription
Short editing and writing jobs
Keyword searches
Photo captioning and tagging

How Mechanical Turk Works:
To begin working for Mechanical Turk, go to the Mechanical Turk website and simply choose to accept a HIT. It will then prompt you to sign into your Amazon.com account or to create one. In taking this step, you agree to the Mechanical Turk privacy notice.
Browse HITs looking for ones that interest you. Examine the "Reward" field to see what it pays. "Time Allotted" tells you how long you have to finish the task before it is considered abandoned and is assigned to someone else. This is not necessarily how long it will take. Many HITs

will give an estimated time for completion in the full description but some do not.

Click on the name of the HIT for a very brief description and click on "View a HIT in this group" to see a full description. On this screen you can choose to accept a HIT or you can skip it and look at other HITs from the same requester.

You can search HITs by keyword or sort them by reward amount or qualifications required.

Payment:
Payments from Mechanical Turk are based on a <u>digital piece work model</u> in which workers receive a fixed fee for each job completed. Because this work is for independent contractors there are no minimum wage protections. Another caution is that requesters may reject work and refuse to pay.

Immediately after a HIT is accepted by the requester, the worker is paid into an Amazon Payments account. However, the time between submitting a HIT to approval can vary from a few hours to a few days.

For U.S.-based workers, money can then be transferred to a U.S. bank account. Workers in India can elect to receive a check in Indian rupees. For all others not based in the U.S. or India, earnings can be transfer to an Amazon gift card.

**Capital Typing** (<u>www.capitaltyping.com</u>)

Outsourcing company based in North Carolina offers a variety of services to its clients and hires freelancers (independent contractors) to perform them. These services include transcription, data entry, market research, translation, online customer support and secretarial services.

Types of Work-at-Home Opportunities at Capital Typing:

As is typical with BPOs, the company hires independent contractors, not employees, for its home-based jobs. Typically independent contractors in these types of positions are paid a <u>per piece rate,</u> e.g. per audio hour transcribed or per word, not an hourly rate, so there is no guarantee of minimum wage.

Listed below are the types of home-based opportunities on the company's website. However, the company may not be hiring all or any of these types of positions at a given time.

- Secretarial services - administrative office support for individuals and large corporations
- Transcription - medical, legal and general transcription, Captioning, movie and TV transcripts
- Data entry - data extraction, research, database development and management, direct mail and marketing services

- Online customer support - email response management, live customer support and chat
- Bilingual - translation, transcription and customer support in Spanish, French and German

The company's website is static, and its job opportunities are vague, indicating that though it isn't necessarily a scam, it may not actually be hiring. This company generates a lot of interest from seekers so I have attempted to research it further.

To Apply to Capital Typing: Upload an application in the form on this page of the Capital Typing website. If you are hired or even get a response from the company

**Clickworker (http://www.clickworker.com/en/)**

Industry:
Data entry, translation and writing, using in a crowd sourcing platform
Company Description:
Global company uses *crowd sourcing* to distribute micro tasks (aka micro labor) in fields such as writing, translating, data entry and research to more than 300,000 "clickworkers" worldwide. The company's clients--which include Honda, Groupon, PayPal and T Mobile--contract with it to have a larger project completed and then Clickworker breaks the project down in to smaller tasks, which can be completed by many different freelance workers.

Types of Work-at-Home Opportunities at Clickworker:
As is typical in crowd sourcing marketplace micro jobs, the freelancers at Clickworker choose small tasks from the pool of available projects. What tasks are available for a freelancer to choose from is based on the qualifications of that freelancer. Qualifications are determined by his or performance on assessments and on previous work completed.

The types of services performed by Clickworker's freelancers for its clients include:
Writing:
SEO text creation and optimization for online marketing
Product descriptions and the categorization of products in e-commerce
Data Entry and research:
Structuring large amounts of data by categorizing and indexing
Categorization and tagging of videos, audio content, image
Address enrichment, data validation and online research for databases
Data verification and research
Translation

Pay and Benefits:
The company states "On average, we expect that a Clickworker earns $9.00 per hour." However, workers are not paid by the hour; payment is on a per piece basis, which means this could vary significantly depending on how fast a freelancer can work. Workers receive a fixed fee for each job completed. According to the company, fees "can range anywhere from a few cents to double-digit Euro sum." The company pays in either Euros or US dollars.

Because Clickworker hires independent contractors, there are no benefits and no guarantee of minimum wage for workers. Payment is made on the 7th or 8th day of the month (or the first non-weekend day after that) for money earned as of the last day of the previous month. You will need to have earned €10 or $10 USD in order for a payment to be processed.

Qualifications and Requirements:
There are very few requirements for Clickworkers. You must be legally able to work in the jurisdiction where you live and have a computer with Internet access. If you live in the United States you must be age 18, but this requirement may vary based on legal age in your country. However, workers must also pass assessments in order to have access to work. The company hires worldwide, but you must have a bank account in a SEPA (Single Euro Payments Area) country or have a valid PayPal account and that can accept payment.

Applying to Clickworkers:
Depending on your language preference, choose the website: Clickworker in English or Clickworker in German. Choose the "For Clickworkers" tab and hit register. Fill out the basic information of name, address and email and agree to the terms of service. You will receive an email with a link to log in to Clickworker. You will then have to take assessments to see which projects you can work on.


**DionData Solutions** (http://www.diondatasolutions.net/opportunities.htm)
Industry:
Data entry
Company Description:
Missouri-based data management firm DionData Solutions uses independent contractors to perform data entry from home, making it one of a fairly small number of legitimate work-at-home data entry companies in an industry filled with data entry scams.

Types of Work-at-Home Opportunities at DionData Solutions:
Data entry independent contractors at DionData enter data from images of documents, often handwritten ones such as applications. The work is compensated on a per-piece basis.

Applying to DionData Solutions:
The DionData Solutions website says it is accepting applications. However, that doesn't necessarily mean it is hiring. This message has not changed for years. Applications are accepted via email only. Though it says it can't respond to all applicants, the company encourages applicants to resubmit after 30 days. Like Axion Data, another legit home data entry company, Dion Data likely keeps a list of possible contractors and hires as needed.

There are no fees to apply or for training.

Qualifications and Requirements:
DionData requires of its home data entry operators: 60 WPM accurate typing skills; basic computer skills, such as sending and receiving email with attachments, using the Internet, uploading and downloading files; the ability to work independently on multiple projects simultaneously; excellent communication skills--written and verbal.

Operators must provide and maintain their own desktop computer (dual monitors is a plus) and a high speed Internet connection (DSL or cable). U.S. citizenship and residency is required.

Pay and Benefits:
All data entry agents are hired as independent contractors which mean there are no benefits and no guarantee of minimum wage. In fact, home data entry jobs very often play less than the minimum wage, especially at the beginning before the data entry worker has developed enough familiarity with the process to work quickly. DionData pays its data entry operators on a per-piece basis, which is typical.


**Driver Guide**
(http://www.flexjobs.com/jobs/telecommuting-jobs-at-driverguide.com)

Driver Guide is an award winning database of thousands of product software drivers, firmware and support documents (manuals) for hundreds of technology products available on the current and past markets. Often hard to find drivers for computer peripherals can be found on Driver Guide thanks to their tireless search and the talents of their IT team. The company continues to experience growth and therefore has multiple opportunities to work from home as a database helper, PHP Developer or Graphic Designer. These positions are part time, with some degree of flexibility available. Training is provided to qualified candidates who are then allowed to work from the comfort of their home as virtual professionals. To find out more about the telecommuting opportunities that Driver Guide can offer you.   Apply for Driver Guide jobs using Flex jobs.

**Virtual Bee** (https://www.virtualbee.com/)
Industry:
Data entry
Company Description:
Lionbridge Technology, Inc., acquired *crowd sourcing* company Virtual Solutions, the parent company of VirtualBee (which changed its name from KeyForCash), in 2012. Virtual Bee uses a workforce of home-based independent contractors to securely enter its client's data, using technology that only allows each of the data entry keyers to see a portion of the confidential original data.

Types of Work-at-Home Opportunities at Virtual Bee:
Home-based data entry operators log on to the Virtual Bee system and choose data entry tasks. They see an image of the data and then must enter it with accuracy. See this video to learn more:
*www.youtube.com/watch?v=EAA9IKuvXSM*

Pay and Benefits:
All data-entry keyers are hired as independent contractors. This means there are no benefits and no guarantee of minimum wage. Payment is on a per piece basis, and different types of data entry pay at different rates. Expect the per-piece rate to work out to about $5-6 per hour.
Pays weekly by check, but the minimum amount paid out is $30. Hours are flexible but there may be certain days of the week or periods during the year when work is not available.

Qualifications and Requirements:
You also must be at least 18 years old to work for Virtual Bee. A score of 97 to 100 percent on the evaluation test is the main qualification of this job.
The company hires worldwide. However, the company divides its workers into two groups--one is for those who reside in the continental 48 United States and the second is for all international individuals (as long as they have maintained a physical presence outside of the United States for the previous 3 consecutive calendar years).
Technical requirements are a computer with an Internet connection and a web browser with JavaScript enabled.

Applying to Virtual Bee:
Click on "Sign Up" on the Virtual Bee website, and then fill in the short form with basic information about yourself. You will then receive an email with a link to a three-part evaluation. This is a test of your data-entry keying ability. It is important that you follow the directions carefully. You will need a score in the high 90s (on a 100-point scale) to

become registered at Virtual Bee. However, you can retake the evaluation once a day until you achieve that score.

It may take 6 to 8 weeks to hear back from Virtual Bee. There are no fees of any kind to work here. However, you may see advertised offers on its website. Participating in these is not required and will not improve your chances of being hired.

**Quicktate** (iDictate) (http://www.quicktate.com/)

Industry:
Data entry, general transcription, medical transcription
Company Description:
Quicktate supports a variety of services and apps that convert short bits of recorded speech into the written word. These include Evernote apps (voicemail messages and audio notes), TweetCall (dictated tweets), CallTroops (phoned letters to military personnel), and Voice on the Go (dictated texts). However, Quicktate and its partner iDictate also offer services for longer transcription projects, which include medical reports, conference calls, and legal files.

Types of Work-at-Home Opportunities at Quicktate or iDictate:
In these micro jobs, data entry operators listen to audio files and transcribe them. The voicemail message files average 1-2 minutes in length, while the other recordings are longer. Hours are flexible and operators can work as many or as few hours as they can handle and/or obtain. In this type of crowd sourcing platform, operators log on to the company's system and claim files to transcribe.

Data entry operators begin at Quicktate and may be promoted to iDictate, which pays more. Quicktate also does medical transcription, which also pays more. Most Quicktate transcription is done in English or Spanish. However, the company also seeks transcribers with skills in French, Italian, German, Chinese, Farsi, Portuguese and Japanese for iDictate projects.

.
Pay and Benefits:
All Quicktate and iDictate's data entry agents are hired as independent contractors. This means there are no benefits and no guarantee of minimum wage.
Quicktate and iDictate pay its data entry operators on a per-word basis. The rate of pay for Quicktate general transcription is $.0025 per word or 4 words for 1 cent, while the rate for Quicktate medical transcription and iDictate work is $.0050 per word or 2 words for 1 cent. This might work

out to $5-7/hour at Quicktate, but keep in mind there is not likely enough work to make this a full-time pursuit.
Payment, which is weekly, is through PayPal account only.

Qualifications and Requirements:
Quicktate seeks professional transcriptionists that follows directions well, have a strong grammar and typing skills, accurate spelling and punctuation and can listen to voice files and accurately type what they hear.
Typists must supply their own equipment, supplies, work space and Internet connection. Computers may be Windows-based or Macs and must have a Firefox, Safari, or Google Chrome browser. Additionally, typists must have a Yahoo IM account and download and install QuickTime. Express Scribe is a free software application that may be useful. A headset, and possibly a foot pedal, may be needed.
All contractors for Quicktate must fill out an electronic W-9 tax form even if they are not located in the United States.

Applying to Quicktate:
To apply, create a typist account by filling out an application on the Quicktate website. Two non-family references are required, and you must answer two short essay questions. (Be sure to use correct grammar and spelling.)
Next applicants should read through the Help Desk FAQ and other postings to become familiar with the procedures. Applicants must then take a quiz that will cover both Quicktate procedures and include an audio file to transcribe. If you wish to be considered for transcription in other languages than English or medical transcription jobs you must complete those audio files.
Expect to wait at least two weeks to hear back from Quicktate. If your application is approved, you will receive a letter. Until then, you will not be able to log in to your account and accept assignments.


**Working Solutions** (www.workingsolutions.com/)

Industry:
Business Process Outsourcing (BPO) that provides inbound technical support, sales and customer service as well as data entry and editing services.
Company Description:
Based in Plano, TX, Working Solutions bills itself as "the first company to utilize an entire workforce of home-based customer sales and service agents." Founded in 1996, the company utilizes independent contractor virtual call center agents, which it calls "Agents On Demand," to services clients' call center needs. Additionally it also hires contractors for data entry work.

Qualifications:
Applicants must be 18 years old. Working Solutions "looks for skilled, educated, and motivated people" to fill its ranks. Agents are required to provide their own computer equipment (with Windows Vista or higher) and Internet service (DSL or cable).

Types of Work-at-Home Positions:
Working Solutions hires independent contractors to work on a project basis in home call centers and on data entry.
Virtual call center agents handle inbound and outbound customer service, sales, market research and/or technical support. These positions could include enrollments, retail sales, reservations, account support and technical assistance on electronics, websites, software and telephony. Agents work with customers over the phone, through online chat and email.
The company also seeks bilingual agents with fluency in Arabic, Bengali, Cantonese, Creole, Filipino, French, French-Canadian, German, Hindi, Italian, Japanese, Korean, Mandarin, Portuguese, Russian, Samoan, Spanish and Vietnamese. Company also hires travel agents with knowledge of Apollo, Amadeus, Galileo, Sabre or WorldSpan and corporate booking experience.

In addition to call center agents Working Solutions hires for *data entry jobs*, which don't involve phone time.

Pay and Benefits:
Because Working Solutions hires independent contractors there is no guarantee of minimum wage or any number of hours per week. However, the position is likely a *part-time call center job*. The company says its projects, which all compensate differently, pay anywhere from $7.50 to $30 an hour. However, they may not necessarily calculate pay on an hourly rate. Agents invoice Working Solutions, based on their projects' pay instructions, and are paid every two weeks.
Again because it hires independent contractors, the company does not offer benefits of any kind. For more information on the distinction between employees and contractors, Agents are able to choose their own hours online. However, the availability of hours can vary making it difficult to earn a full-time living at Working Solutions. Despite their status as independent contractors, agents aren't charged any fees by the company.

Geographic Restrictions:
The company hires Agents OnDemand in all U.S. states and from across the world. However the number of projects, particularly call center jobs, for residents outside the U.S. is more limited.

Applying to Working Solutions:
Submit an application online through the company's website. You may paste a resume into the comments field of the application. At the end of the online application, you will be asked to answer a few questions in part one of an assessment. Multiple choice and written-answer questions will test your knowledge of customer service as well as assess your grammar and writing skills.

After submitting this, you will be able to complete the second part of the assessment. For this you will call in and record answers regarding customer service scenarios. After this your application will be evaluated and you will be notified if your application will be placed in the "pending pool," meaning that you will be considered for opportunities that match your qualifications. If there is a match you will be contacted by email. It can take several weeks to months to be matched with the first project.

**Writers Research Group**
(http://www.writersresearchgroup.com/company/jobs.html)

We are always in search of talented, self-motivated, detail-oriented professionals capable of meeting strict client specifications and tight deadlines.
We offer a range of exciting opportunities:
*Data Entry Specialists* input a variety of data for a wide range of projects. Quick, accurate typing and attention-to-detail are a must for this position.

**Cass Information Systems**
(http://www.cassinfo.com/Corporate/Careers/Job-Openings/COL-Offsite-Invoice-Payment-Specialist.aspx)

Job position: Offsite Invoice Payment Specialist
Primary position responsibilities
Operate and maintain a PC in a work-at-home environment

Accurately enter data to pay utility invoices and prepare customized reports

Perform required steps dictated by online programs and procedures

Knowledge and minimum requirements

Must be able to key a minimum of 9,000 KSPH, both alpha and numeric combined

Candidates must have good analytical and problem-solving skills and be dependable and quality minded

Training will be done in the office Monday through Friday 9:00 AM – 2:00 PM for approximately 90 days. The home schedule is a minimum of 20-25 hours over Saturday/Sunday, Monday, Tuesday and Friday.

Location: Columbus, Ohio

# EDITING/WRITING

**About.com** (http://experts.about.com/)

Those freelancers who are most successful writing for About.com are highly skilled, self-motivated, and experienced web content creators with a deep passion for their topic area and impeccable journalistic integrity. They create original and easy-to-consume articles to meet the diverse needs that arise in readers' everyday lives; are able to produce content on a regular basis on their own time; and have the entrepreneurial spirit and conviction necessary to build independently upon their expertise and authority.

About.com contracts with more than 100 experts in many different fields. They write online content from home and are paid a minimum based on the number of articles they create. However, compensation increases with page view growth.

**Allvoices** (www.allvoices.com)

Writers are paid based on the performance of their "brand" or page views of the news content they write. Payment is based on page views and contributors are paid in minimum $100 increments.

As the world's premier platform for citizen journalism, Allvoices is committed to delivering a community-driven platform for open, global news and idea exchange. In support of this mission, Allvoices:

Empowers contributors around the world to share news and views Fosters an engaged community of contributors and audience members who value critical thinking and intelligent discourse while remaining respectful of one another rewards contributors financially for the page views their content generates in a regular and reliable fashion delivers technology solutions that help contributors gain exposure and build a following provides contributors with resources to help their stories stand out, including licensed photos, writing tips from other members of the community and social media tools helps contributors improve their writing voice and gain valuable experience and mentoring by enabling mentoring exchanges with other contributors. Responds quickly and effectively to users' flags of inappropriate content.

**ChaCha** (http://becomeaguide.chacha.com/)

Like a search engine but with live work-at-home guides answering the questions, ChaCha pays per answer, which it says averages out to $3-9 per hour.

**Clickworker** (http://www.clickworker.com/en/)

Industry:
Data entry, translation and writing, using in a crowd sourcing platform
Company Description:
Global company uses _crowd sourcing_ to distribute micro tasks (aka _micro labor_) in fields such as writing, translating, data entry and research to more than 300,000 "clickworkers" worldwide. The company's clients--which include Honda, Groupon, PayPal and T Mobile--contract with it to have a larger project completed and then Clickworker breaks the project down in to smaller tasks, which can be completed by many different freelance workers.

Types of Work-at-Home Opportunities at Clickworker:
As is typical in crowd sourcing marketplace _micro jobs_, the freelancers at Clickworker choose small tasks from the pool of available projects. What tasks are available for a freelancer to choose from is based on the qualifications of that freelancer. Qualifications are determined by his or performance on assessments and on previous work completed.

The types of services performed by Clickworker's freelancers for its clients include:
Writing:
SEO text creation and optimization for online marketing
Product descriptions and the categorization of products in e-commerce
Data Entry and research:
Structuring large amounts of data by categorizing and indexing
Categorization and tagging of videos, audio content, image
Address enrichment, data validation and online research for databases
Data verification and research
Translation

Pay and Benefits:
The company states "On average, we expect that a Clickworker earns $9.00 per hour." However, workers are not paid by the hour; payment is on a per piece basis, which means this could vary significantly depending on how fast a freelancer can work. Workers receive a fixed fee for each job completed. According to the company, fees "can range anywhere from a few cents to double-digit Euro sum." The company pays in either Euros or US dollars.
Because Clickworker hires independent contractors, there are no benefits and no guarantee of minimum wage for workers.
Payment is made on the 7th or 8th day of the month (or the first non-weekend day after that) for money earned as of the last day of the previous month. You will need to have earned €10 or $10 USD in order for a payment to be processed.

Qualifications and Requirements:
There are very few requirements for Clickworkers. You must be legally able to work in the jurisdiction where you live and have a computer with Internet access. If you live in the United States you must be age 18, but this requirement may vary based on legal age in your country. However, workers must also pass assessments in order to have access to work.

The company hires worldwide, but you must have a bank account in a SEPA (Single Euro Payments Area) country or have a valid PayPal account and that can accept payment.
Applying to Clickworkers:
Depending on your language preference, choose the website: Clickworker in English or Clickworker in German. Choose the "For Clickworkers" tab and hit register. Fill out the basic information of name, address and email and agree to the terms of service. You will receive an email with a link to log in to Clickworker. You will then have to take assessments to see which projects you can work on.

Worldwide crowd sourcing company hires independent contractors for writing jobs as well as data entry, translation, and research. Pays on a per piece basis. Registration and an assessment are necessary before "clickworkers" can begin accepting tasks for payments.

**Crowd sourcing**: (http://www.cloudcrowd.com/)

Crowd sourcing company offers micro jobs in general writing, marketing writing, and editing (Chicago Manual of Style). Writers and editors sign up using Facebook. They must pass a series of assessment and build a credibility score to access each type of work, which each pay a small fee and possibly a bonus.

**Demand Studios** (http://create.demandstudios.com/join-us/)

Demand Studios accepts applicants with writing, editing and filmmaking skills. They are assigned to produce made-for-the-Internet content that appear on sites like eHow.com, LIVESTRONG.COM and dozens more sites. Writers are paid both on a flat fee and revenue sharing basis.

**Examiner** (http://www.examiner.com/About_Examiner)

Writing jobs at Examiner.com are for writers with insights and knowledge about local events and communities in topics ranging from sports and parenting to food and green living. Pay is based on the size of your readership.

**Hub Pages** (http://hubpages.com/)

HubPages bills itself as the "leading online publishing ecosystem." Writers sign up and publish their work. Revenue from Adsense and affiliates is split with HubPages, which receives a 40 percent share.

**Internet Brands** (http://www.internetbrands.com/ib/careersdivision/)

Internet media company that operates community and e-commerce web sites in the automotive, careers, home, shopping, and travel and leisure categories hires telecommuting writers and editors.

**Mahalo** (http://www.mahalo.com/mahalo-freelance-writer-positions/)

Mahalo calls itself "a human-powered search engine dedicated to delivering carefully curated search results featuring the highest quality, spam-free links available." It hires freelance writers for $10-12 an hour for a minimum of 20 hours a week to fulfill this mission.

**Pro-Blogger** (http://jobs.problogger.net/)

The ProBlogger Job Board is where bloggers looking for jobs and companies looking to hire bloggers meet.

**Quarasan** (http://tbe.taleo.net/CH04/ats/careers/jobSearch.jsp?org=QUARASAN&cws=1)

Educational publisher offers editing and writing jobs that can be done from home.

**Smart Brief** (http://www.smartbrief.com/)

Discover a work experience where diverse ideas are met with enthusiasm, and where you can learn and grow to your full potential. We're looking for individuals who enjoy the entrepreneurial thrill of invention and who enjoy working as a team to create a satisfying outcome for our customers.

SmartBrief hires editors, often as part-time telecommuters, to comb through the day's business news stories from a wide range of sources and distill the news related to a specific industry into a daily newsletter.

**Suite 101** (http://www.examiner.com/article/suite-101-offers-freelance-writing-jobs)

Suite101 is an online magazine written by freelancers who are experts in many fields. Writers must submit 10 articles in every three month and are paid based on ad revenues for their work.

**Textbroker** (http://www.textbroker.com/)

Textbroker.com is exactly what the name implies: It's a site which acts as a broker between individuals or companies that need a bit of writing done and freelancers who will gladly spit out 200-400 words or so for pay. Texbroker.com rates your writing sample on a general scale of 2-5, with a "5" rating reserved for professional writers.

**The Content Authority** (http://thecontentauthority.com/)

The Content Authority, commonly referred to as TCA, is very similar to Textbroker in terms of topics and pay rates. They also have four tiers of writers with rates ranging from $.007 per word to $.03 per word. The minimum amount earned for payout is higher, at $25, but the pay is still weekly. They pay each Monday via PayPal.

**Interact Media** (http://www.interactmedia.com/writers-faq/)

Interact Media has several more levels, each with higher pay rates. They range from $.007 cent to $.16 per word. They pay via PayPal twice per month on the 1$^{st}$ and 15$^{th}$. The most glaring difference between Interact Media and Textbroker is that the editors only review your first article, after that all reviews and even ratings come from the clients. The rating system is similar, from 1 to 5 stars. Also, clients have the option of offering "tips" for material they consider to be worthy of more than the price originally charged.

**Writer's Domain** (https://www.writersdomain.net/)

Writer's Domain is another site that offers a job board with fairly broad topics to write on. Most of their jobs are fairly uniform in that they are required to be around 250 to 300 words and include the keyword two times. Pay is $3 for each article from 250 to 300 words. Ratings are done by editors, and each article receives from 1 to 5 stars on both content and grammar. Those who get 4 or 5 stars on grammar get a $.30 bonus on that article. This means you could easily make $3.30 for one 250 to 300 word article. They pay via PayPal once per month, on the 5$^{th}$. However, once you hit $100 in earnings you have the option to click a "pay me now" button and get paid right then. Another big difference here is that, in addition to a writing sample being required for the application, there is also a basic grammar test. Writer's Domain is tightening up on their content requirements beginning in September 2012, so be aware of that also.

**MediaPiston** (http://www.pistonagency.com/who-we-are/careers)

Media Piston offers jobs on a job board, and you pick what you want to write about. However, most have much more detailed instructions than other content sites. The tradeoff is that most of the jobs pay significantly more. Work is not available as often, but at least weekly it is possible to pick up a job or two. Once an article is approved by the client, you get paid via PayPal. Clients here also have the option to pay a "bonus" for what they consider to be great content. We're always on the lookout for smart, talented people that can help make Piston even better. Storytellers, eggheads, artists, techies, trend spotters, social butterflies and beyond; People with as much life experience as work experience; People that have a passion for marketing, a strong work ethic, and an insatiable curiosity work on our team. Around here, we work at the intersection of commerce, culture, and technology – an approach that has inspired a bunch of award-winning ideas.

**Scripted** (https://scripted.com/writers/sign_up)

Scripted offers significantly higher pay, but they have fewer jobs and topics to choose from. You have to apply for each category you wish to be allowed to accept jobs from, but once you are in you can make anywhere from $10 up to however much a client is willing to pay for one blog post. Also, they often send out private emails to writers who do well on certain topics, offering to let them accept jobs before they are posted on the job board.

When you write for Scripted, you are a ghostwriter for their clients who are in need of content, so you don't get your name published on what you create and all rights to the content are transferred over to the client upon article acceptance.

## Payment at Scripted

The amount you earn will vary depending on a lot of different things including the type of content, the length, and the topic, but from what I understand there are many assignments that pay upwards of $20 a piece.

Scripted states that you can expect payment for the content you create bimonthly, on the 15th and last day of each month. Payments will be made via Bill.com beginning in April 2013. The company has decided to move away from PayPal.

If you are asked to do edits, Scripted promises to pay within two days after the edits are completed and approved. If their clients reject your edits, you will still be paid 50 percent so your work won't have been for nothing.

## The Application Process

To begin writing for Scripted, you have to fill out the writer registration form and also submit a writing sample (one that has never been previously published). If you are in the U.S. you will also need to fill out a W-9 (you are considered an independent contractor for Scripted.) You are free to apply if you live outside the U.S., and of course the W-9 is not required if you are not a U.S. resident.

When you apply, you must select different industries you feel you are qualified to write in and a sample reflecting your ability to write within each industry you select is required. So if you select three different industries, you'll need to submit three different samples for each one. The current industries you can choose from are art and design, business and finance, internet and software, environmental, government and politics, law and legal, lifestyle and travel, media and entertainment, and sports and fitness. You may only apply to each specialty once. If you get rejected for an industry, you can't ever attempt to apply to it again.

After you've been approved, you'll see that you have a writer score that is assigned to you based on the quality of the sample(s) you submitted when you signed up. The higher the score, the better because sometimes writers with high scores get a chance to claim jobs before writers with lower scores do. Also, you might get more email invites if your score is high.

## Grabbing Assignments

Once your application has been approved and you are officially in the system, you should be able to see by logging in some jobs that are available within each industry you got approved for. Scripted also occasionally sends out email invites letting you know when something is open that they think you would be a good fit to write.

Clients can additionally "favorite" you if they really like your writing, then this will give you first dibs on assignments from those clients.

**Caption Colorado**
(http://www.captioncolorado.com/captioning-careers)

Caption Colorado offers full and part-time captioning positions and a world where competitive rates, flexible hours, technical support, 401K, flex spending accounts, health/dental/vision and training are all available from the comfort and convenience of your home. And, on top of that, wouldn't it be great to know that what you do every day has tremendous value and purpose.

Our captioners deliver the missing soundtrack and provide access to what's happening in the world, and you can too! Trading in your shoes may be easier than you think…

Am I ready to be a Caption Colorado Realtime Captioner?
You're Ready if You Are…
A clean, complete, and consistent writer with 98+% accuracy.
A writer who is conflict-free and uses prefixes, suffixes, etc. in your writing style.
A team player who is able to work within Caption Colorado's policies, procedures, and guidelines.
A reliable and punctual person who is dedicated to delivering exceptional customer service.

A writer who actively seeks ways to develop and maintain superior real time captioning skills through self-correcting, continuing education, and a willingness to give, receive, and incorporate feedback…..then apply.

Your application will be screened and selected candidates will be invited to take a real time assessment, which consists of a 30 minute local news program. When an opening becomes available, candidates with the top assessment scores will be interviewed and candidate selection will be based on the assessment score and the final interview. Assessments are reviewed on the basis of keystroke accuracy, conflicts, word boundary problems, overall flow, completeness, and comprehensibility. Candidates may be asked to complete more than one assessment.

**Writers Research Group**
(http://www.writersresearchgroup.com/company/jobs.html)

We are always in search of talented, self-motivated, detail-oriented professionals capable of meeting strict client specifications and tight deadlines.

We offer a range of exciting opportunities:
Writers provide material for one or more of a variety of nonfiction and technical projects, including technical manuals, training or instructional manuals, nonfiction books, literary criticisms, academic reference materials, directory listings, and web pages.

*Editors* provide one or more of the three levels of copyediting (Primary, Intermediate, and Advanced). The level of editing will vary depending on each individual project and may include work on reference and nonfiction books, technical and academic materials, directory listings, and corporate or small business websites.

*Researchers* provide data for one or more of a variety of ongoing projects, including directory listings, literary criticisms, and biographical, nonfiction, technical, or academic reference materials using Internet, phone, fax, email, and/or library research.

If you are interested in any of these positions, email your resume to: info@writersresearchgroup.com.
Writers Research Group does not discriminate in employment on the basis of race, color, national origin, age, sex, sexual orientation, disability, veteran or marital status, or other protected status covered by federal, state, or local law.

**Wise Geek** (https://www.wisegeek.com/freelance-writing-jobs.htm)

No Deadlines: Write Whenever you Want
As a WiseGEEK writer, you'll be able to login to our system whenever you want; set your own hours and work whenever it fits into your schedule.

  *Write from Anywhere
WiseGEEK writers can work from anywhere they have an internet connection. You'll be able to work at a cafe, in the yard, at a library, or from your kitchen table.

  *Choose your Topics
Our writers get to choose their favorite topics from an open pool of at least 500 topics. These topics, always in the form of a question, span a broad range of categories, including finance, technology, legal, beauty, diets, nutrition, fitness, medicine, fashion, gardening and more! You'll be free to focus on the one or many categories that you are comfortable writing about.

*Work Directly with your Own Editor

Each WiseGEEK writer is assigned to a dedicated, experienced and receptive editor. You'll get to work directly with your editor to hone your skills and build your writing portfolio, all while getting paid!

*Educate Millions of People

WiseGEEK is read by over 15.5 Million people each month (well over 100 million visitors per year). Your articles will help lots of real people, sometimes in very significant ways.

Writers choose from a pool of available topics and write articles for a rate of $10-$14 per article. Five articles per week or 20 a month are expected. Articles are edited, and a byline is given. Payment is through PayPal.

**Indeed.com** (http://about.indeed.com/jobs/freelance-writer)

Search "freelance writer"

**hirewriters.com** (http://www.hirewriters.com/signup/writer)

If English is your first language, join HireWriters.com today for FREE and you will have access to HUNDREDS of paid writing jobs. Clients post writing assignments and you can then accept the job and get paid when you complete it!

**blogmunchies.com** (http://blogmunchies.com/write-for-us/)

If you think you have what it takes to *write* for *BlogMunchies* submit a sample ... forms part of *BlogMunchies*.com terms and conditions, by submitting articles to *us* for ... Please see these *blog* post guidelines for an example of how we like our submissions.

**goarticles.com** (http://goarticles.com/author.html)

This is only an internet marketing avenue and does not pay the author directly. The author can write the article and submit to goarticles.com in order to bring more attention to their service/product website.

**zerys.com** (http://www.zerys.com/writers/)

Interact Media's Zerys platform gives you the opportunity to earn steady side income, doing what you love... all from the comfort of your own home.

- No monthly fees
- No need to purchase bid credits - get unlimited access to writing jobs

- No need to submit bid proposals
- Get notified when new jobs are posted that match your profile
- Develop long-term relationships with clients and build a steady source of work

**contentcurrent.com** (http://www.contentcurrent.com/write)

We are currently hiring determined contract writers for article writing and custom writing tasks. By joining ContentCurrent, you have the opportunity to work the hours you want and get paid every week. As a ContentCurrent writer, you will be able to pick the writing tasks that suit your skills and/or interests and submit them through our easy-to-use interface. There are hundreds of writing tasks waiting to be completed on ContentCurrent.

**allcustomcontent.com** (http://www.allcustomcontent.com/work-from-home/)

We are currently looking for serious-minded freelancers to provide assistance in our growing content providing and transcribing business.

We are currently looking for talented and detail-oriented writers with an excellent command of the written English language.

Positions Available: Freelance positions ghostwriting articles, reports, e-books and other content. We are also looking for writers to be able to rewrite transcriptions and other documents to put them in a useable format for end-users.

Potential for Growth: There may be future opportunities to become a Senior Writer or a Team Leader. Both positions include more available work and increased rates of pay.

Writing Skills & Qualifications: Please read through these qualifications to ensure this position is right for you.

- Some Experience: It is not required that you have written as a professional or freelance writer for clients before. We are more concerned with quality writing and will ask you to conduct a writing exercise during the application process.
- Research Skills: Your writing projects will, in some cases, require initial research and will be focused on topics easily searched for on the Internet. More technical writing will only be provided to you if you indicate you already have a knowledge base in that particular area.
- Ability to Adjust Writing Style: The projects you receive will range from formal to casual writing styles. You must be able to adapt to those styles where required and outlined in each project description.

- Ability to Learn Industry Jargon: Writing projects will be on a number of different topics. You don't need to understand all jargon prior to starting, but you will need to be able to research terminology or ask for help, when needed.
- Nonfiction Writing Only: We are only looking for nonfiction writers to write and rewrite informational content. We are not looking for fiction writing at this time.

General Skills and Attributes You Must Have:

- Detail Oriented: You will be responsible for editing and proofreading your work prior to submission and must pay close attention to details.
- Be Willing to Accept Constructive Feedback: To provide the best service possible to our clients and in order to keep bringing you more work, you must be able to accept and adapt to the constructive feedback provided to you.
- Excellent Communication Skills: As a freelancer, you will be in regular communication with your Team Leader who is responsible for timely and quality service delivery to our clients. Your communication must facilitate this process for your Team Leader.
- Commitment to Quality Client Service: You must respect deadlines and complete projects that you accept from us.
- Maintain Confidentiality: Client confidentiality is of utmost importance in working with All Custom Content. Any breach of confidentiality will result in the termination of your contract.

**ProficientWriters.com**
(http://www.proficientwriters.com/writing-at-home)

Creative people seldom march to the same drummer as those with jobs that don't require those same abilities. One of the reasons that employers appreciate good freelance writers is that they don't require much supervision. ProficientWriters.com only wants people who are capable of writing at home and delivering good content in the timeframe agreed upon.

**wordy.com** (https://wordy.com/wordy-for-editors/)

Wordy is a real-time, human, copy-editing and proofreading service for everything you write. Wordy optimizes the accuracy, consistency and readability of content from Fortune 500 business reports to website copy. As an editor on Wordy we expect you to have an excellent, professional working knowledge of the language, grammar, usage, punctuation and standard editorial conventions (e.g. New Hart's Rules, Chicago Manual of Style, etc.).

**blogmutt.com** (https://www.blogmutt.com/pages/writer)
Blogmutt serves businesses that have websites with blogs, and the people there just don't have the time or writing talent to fill up that blog them.

Our system is more straightforward than any of the content farms:

1. You write posts for businesses.
2. If they like and use those posts then you get paid.

   The customers get their pick of posts, but they have an ongoing need for original content, so even if your post doesn't get used the first week, most posts eventually get picked. Our acceptance rate right now is at about 90 percent.

   We also give you tools so you will have the best opportunity to write posts that our customers will love.

   Within the Blogmutt platform we have a point system. You earn points for posting, for posts that get picked and for a variety of other internal goals. As you earn points you move up in levels. At certain levels you earn status, such as an exclusive, invite-only LinkedIn honor for success as a professional writer. At higher levels you'll become part of an elite group of writers that gets access to higher-paying work.

**Resume Edge.com**
(http://www.resumeedge.com/work-for-us/amyharrop.com)

About Us ResumeEdge provides professional resume writing and editing services for job seekers worldwide. We are the leading provider of resume writing services and have written and edited thousands of resumes over the years. ResumeEdge is owned and operated by Nelnet, a publicly traded education services company. Nelnet helps students and families plan, prepare, and pay for their education—and find jobs after they graduate from college.

About the Job
You will write and edit resumes, cover letters, and LinkedIn® Profiles using customers' existing resumes and additional information submitted via a questionnaire. You will interact with customers using a ResumeEdge-provided email address. Some assignments will require telephone interviews with clients; calling cards are provided. Self-paced, ongoing training resources are available on our online resume writer portal.

Requirements
Writers must have a strong background in one or more of our 40 job industries or have past experience writing and editing resumes and cover letters. Certified Professional Resume Writers (CPRW) and National

Certified Resume Writers (NCRW) certification is preferred, but not required. Our writing standards are high; ResumeEdge holds all writers to a proprietary certification process that includes adhering to quarterly quality checks. You must have access to a computer and the Internet, and be an expert in Microsoft Word. Excellent verbal and written communication, patience, data organization, and critical thinking skills required. Benefits As a freelance resume writer, you have the flexibility to work from anywhere. You set your own hours and schedule and take as few or as many assignments as you like. ResumeEdge writers may also accept/continue freelance assignments with other businesses. Pay is per assignment; bonuses are available for resume writers with excellent customer feedback.

How to Apply
If you meet the above requirements, we'd love to hear from you. Submit your resume and a "before" and "after" of a resume you've edited or written. If selected for further evaluation, you will be contacted via email. The evaluation process includes a resume edit, critique, and phone interview.

**articlesmasters.com**
(http://articlesmasters.com/the-writers-at-content-writing-services)

The writers at content writing services follow certain specific formats, such as 12pt Times New Roman font, double spacing and one inch margins on all sides. These are the requirements of most academic assignments and are in accordance with APA formatting. The versatility in prices at content writing services offers clients the option to choose a payment plan that fulfills their requirements.

Writers generally post their sample writings at content writing services or when they apply for a specific job to ensure the client that they have relevant experience. The client can also ask for a sample article or a small portion of their writing project before they hire a writer so that there is better understanding of what each side needs in terms of writing, format, vocabulary and style.

**tongal.com** (http://tongal.com/home)

An ideal opportunity to let your creativity soar --- it is a website that accepts your idea, pitch the idea and if the idea is accepted, you get more support and compensation follows after the project is completed.

**iwriter.com** (http://www.iwriter.com/signup.php)

Sign up below and start earning money by writing articles for other people.

Anyone can register and start earning money immediately. Earn up to $15.00 for every article you write!

**triond.com** (triond.com)

*Triond* publishes user generated content on a network of websites, enabling users to reach a wider audience, gain more recognition and earn more revenue.

**articlecity.com** (www.articlecity.com)
To boost website traffic only. There is no pay to the writer.

**isnare.com** (isnare.com)
To boost website traffic only. There is no pay to the writer.

**Constant-content.com**
(https://www.constant-content.com/area/registerauthor.htm)

Constant-Content attracts professional Web content writers who care about quality and uniqueness as much as you do. With strict quality controls in place, we are able to offer custom content writing services and a huge catalog of Web content and articles written by writers who thoroughly know their craft.

All content writers must pass a screening quiz before their work will be considered. From there, every article and every page of website content submitted undergoes an extensive editorial review. Content writers must consistently submit quality Internet content in order to remain a part of our article writing service. With extensive editorial guidelines and high writing standards in place, only those with exceptional article writing skills and a commitment to providing unique, original content make the cut.

**contently.com** (https://contently.com/journalists)
A website company that promotes freelance writers and publishers.

**wildjunket.com**
(http://www.wildjunket.com/magazine/editorial-guidelines/)

Destination Features: Inspirational first-person, narrative accounts of your travel experience through a country/region – examples include trekking through the Amazon Jungle and traveling overland in Central Asia. The piece should encompass all-rounded aspects of travel: adventure, culture and history. The anecdote should be entertaining and informative.

- Photos: 10-15

- Writing: 1,800-2,200 words including boxes and sidebar
- Payment: US$150
- Sidebar: Getting There, Getting Around, When to Go, Cost of Travel, Packing and Accommodation

Photo Essay: Using striking, high-quality photos to showcase a destination or culture. Whether they are portrait shots of people in Nigeria, landscapes images of Antarctica or wildlife snapshots from the Galapagos Islands, they should piece together to tell a story.

- Photos: 15-20
- Writing: Introduction (400words) and short captions for each selected photo
- Payment: US$80

Travel Guide: A practical guide on a destination with a general introduction, list of must-see attractions and suggestions of up to 5 itineraries around the country. Itineraries can be themed (wildlife, culture, cities etc.) or based on geographical locations (north, central, south etc.) The style should be lively but informative. Include how long each itinerary takes, and what type of traveler it caters to.

- Photos: 10-15
- Writing: 1,800-2,200 words including boxes, sidebar and list of must-sees
- Payment: US$150
- Sidebar: Getting There, Getting Around, When to Go, Cost of Travel, Packing and Accommodation

Dispatches/ Just Back: Short first-person narratives of an unusual experience such as coasteering in Wales or staying in a temple in South Korea (narrower scope than destination feature).

- Photos: 8-10
- Writing: 1,300-1,500 words
- Payment: US$80
- Sidebar: Getting There, When to Go and Accommodation

**Under the Radar**: A short feature on a country/region that has yet to be discovered by mass tourism and have reasons to be in the tourist limelight. This is a general overview of what to see and most of all, why go now. Style should be factual but lively and includes some narratives.

- Photos: 8-10
- Writing: 1,300-1,500 words
- Payment: US$80

- Sidebar: Getting There, When to Go, Must-See Attractions

<u>Feast:</u> Stories that bring you on a journey through a country's gastronomy. Story scopes range from street food in Seoul to bizarre eats of Marrakech to award-winning tapas joints in Barcelona. It should be narrative and quirky yet informative.

- Photos: 8-10
- Writing: 1,000-1,200 words
- Payment: US$50

<u>Smart Travel:</u> This section discusses travel-related topics: from tipping to couch surfing. Article should be thought-provoking and evocative.

- No photos needed
- Writing: 700 words
- No payment

<u>Snapshots:</u> On the first few pages of our magazine, we feature contributions from readers who are interested in showcasing their photos. We look for very striking and outstanding images of landscape, people or culture. Photos must be landscape oriented and bigger than 4MB.

- Writing: A 200-word explanation of how, when and where you took the photo
- No payment

GENERAL GUIDELINES

All articles are written in American English. Prices should also be stated in local currency and USD.

- Please include sub-headings and boxes (at least 1 per feature).
- An author's bio and headshot will be included on the magazine's first page. Please keep
- your bio short (2-3 sentences).
- Articles should be submitted in a Word document and high-res photos (either in RAW or
- jpg of at least 4MB) via *YouSendIt.com*.

PUBLISHING RIGHTS

- Contributors will retain the rights to your articles or photographs.
- Please state if the article or photographs you're pitching are original or have been
- published previously. While we do not have a first run only policy, please assure that all

- parties involved are aware of the republication.

## QUERY PROCESS

Once you've read through our past issues to get a good understanding of the style we're looking for, please send us a brief query summarizing the scope of your story with a proper title, subheading and bullet point summary of the content.

Please include links to photos that would accompany your story or send us low-res versions of the photos. It's advisable to include your credentials and samples of your previous writings or blog links to give us an idea of your writing style.

## CONTACT DETAILS

For all magazine pitches, please contact *Nellie Huang* at editor@wildjunket.com.

**Article world.net** (http://www.articleworld.net/pages/Author-Guidelines)
A website company that promotes freelance writers and publishers.

**ArticleZ.com** (http://www.articlez.com/)
A website company that allows articles to be submitted as a means to drive traffic to website.

**Copypress.com** (http://community.copypress.com/work-with-us/)
CopyPress Community is place where creative's collaborate and work together. CopyPress frequently works with certified marketers on a variety of paid assignments in the following departments:

<u>Writing</u>

CopyPress utilizes a team of trained writers to produce large scale, quality-content campaigns for clients in a variety of industries.

We are always accepting applications from writers interested in receiving paid assignments. All CopyPress writers must:

- Have a high-level knowledge of grammar and writing mechanics
- Have a strong command of the English language
- Be able to construct clear, well-written copy
- Be able to follow directions to accomplish defined editorial objectives
- Be reliable and dependable

Design

CopyPress utilizes a team of talented designers to produce infographics, videos, and illustrations for a variety of industries and platforms.

We are looking to add talented designers to our team. If you are a designer, artist, videographer, or illustrator interested in producing high-quality online media, we want you on our team. CopyPress Community is a learning center, training facility, multimedia educational portal, all rolled into one. This free training portal is for all online marketers (writers, designers, publishers, and everything in between) who want to join the Content Revolution.

**ecopywriters.com**
(http://www.ecopywriters.com/about/employment.html)

ECOPYWRITERS prides itself on hiring only the very best talent. Our company is made up of a vast network of freelance copywriters and our operations team located in San Diego, California.
Our standard employment package includes a base salary plus a discretionary performance bonus. Additionally, we provide health insurance and three weeks paid vacation per year for salaried employees.

**Resmatic**
(http://www.resmatic.net/resmaticinc/detail.php?id=34)

We have an ongoing need for HTML coders working offsite on a CONTRACT basis.
•Hand-write basic, clean html code on a contract basis.
Work with designers and customer reps to make modifications and updates to existing and new client's websites.
•Use your internet skills to search and compile information from the web.

Qualifications:
•This is a telecommuting opportunity. You'll need your own computer, workspace and internet connection.
• You have experience succeeding at projects as a freelance contributor.
•Mastery of html, Photoshop, and working knowledge of installing and configuring pre-written per scripts.
•Knowledge of pier and JavaScript a plus.
•This is a contract "as-needed" position that requires that you be reachable during normal business hours.

**Bubblews** (http://www.bubblews.com/account/create)

So Bubblews is basically an article writing website, where you can write almost about anything under some general categories such as Art, Beauty,

Business, Entertainment, Fashion, and Food etc. Their motto is "Speak Freely. Write Your World". And like most of the content writing websites, you will get paid for number of views you get on your posts. But wait, that is not all...

Bubblews has also given us the chance to monetize our content even further. Bubblews also pays for EVERY comment you get on your post (you won't get paid for comments you make on other's posts-because let's be real, if such an option was there Bubblews would be the most spammed website on the Internet).

Bubblews doesn't stop there. They also pay us for Facebook likes and other shares on social media that our posts receive. You yourself can try and get likes or shares, but the posts will naturally receive likes and shares if the community likes them.

Oh, almost forgot, Bubblews also has a rating system where registered users can 'thumbs up' or 'thumbs down' each post you make. I'm not really sure if this gets you paid directly, but it will certainly improve your post's visibility within the Bubblews community and on the Internet.

The Bubblews community is a patent pending system that enables our users to enjoy our community (without a cost) and share in the ad revenue growth. In fact our revenue model is simple: We split the ad revenue we make off each post with the author 50/50. You will get paid for every view, comment, like/dislike and social media share that your posts gather. Write Your World. Speak Freely. Join the movement


**CyberEdit, Inc. - ResumeEdge.com**
(http://www.writejobs.info/2012/03/freelance-writing-cyber-edit-resume.html)

Lawrenceville, NJ

Contact: Darlene Zambruski

Email: jobs@cyberedit.com

Location: Work From Home

Job Description: Professional resume writers and editors wanted for all shifts, including weekend work -- Friday - Sunday

* Make $35 and upper job
* Work From Home From Anywhere in the World
* Telecommute
* Choose Your Hours (10 - 40 hours per week)
* You Can Begin Now

Creative writing talent wanted. ResumeEdge writers work from their own home or office from anywhere in the world via the Internet 7 days a week.

You would help our IT, Engineering, and tech industry clients write and edit their resumes and cover letters using their existing resumes and cover letters (if available), a phone conversation (we pay for the calls), and information submitted over online forms. This is challenging work requiring a strong knowledge of the IT & Engineering fields.

ResumeEdge provides the resume writing services to thousands of sites, including The Wall Street Journal`s Career Journal, Lycos, SallieMae, and Wet Feet. We are the net's premier resume writing service because of our talented resume writers.

Education: College Degree (or equivalent work experience) in IT (all fields) and/or Engineering (all fields), and/or tech industry (all fields).

EXPERIENCE: REQUIREMENTS

- 2 + years professional experience
- BA or higher (or equivalent professional experience)
- Ability to meet/beat deadlines
- Certified Professional Resume Writers (CPRW) and Nationally Certified Resume Writers (NCRW) are preferred
- Expert in MS Word

Please do not apply unless you have knowledge and/or experience in the IT, Engineering fields or the tech industry and are an expert in Word. Writers with weekend availability are also preferred.

Hours: 10 - 50 hours per week. Flexible Hours.

Salary: $35 and more per job

How To Apply: To apply, please submit your resume (in Word as an attachment, no pdfs, please), cover letter, and one `before` and `after` example of a resume you have edited or written (if available) using this link.

After we review your material, we will email selected applicants with one test resume that requires editing and allows us to make final decisions. Given the large number of applicants, we ask that you please not follow up regarding this job by phone or email until you are selected to take the test.

To begin application process, please submit your resume here.

Please only use the above link to submit your information.

Location: Lawrenceville NJ

Compensation: $35 and more per job

CONTACT INFORMATION:

For inquiries: jobs@cyberedit.com

For submissions: apply here

Website: http://www.cyberedit.com

**Edit Fast**
(http://editfast.com/english/editjobs.htm)

We need you because you are a skilled proofreader, editor, or writer. Edit Fast takes pride in the quality of the work we do and in the speed of our editors. We want the best!

This is a freelance opportunity. We cannot guarantee that there will be work available, but if you have the qualifications Edit Fast's clients are looking for, and if you are patient, there may be projects for you in the future. You should be aware, however, that Edit Fast has no obligation to provide work for you now or at any time in the future. Completing the registration process and passing the Edit Fast review does not necessarily mean you will receive projects. It simply means you are eligible to receive projects and your Web page is available for Edit Fast's clients to view and perhaps choose you as their editor. If you are selected for a project by a client or by the Edit Fast administration you will be notified and that project will be directed to you.

Only those editors who's Web pages have been activated are eligible to receive New Project Notifications. For those who are not successful, all information connected to your email address will be deleted, and notification of this will be sent (This can take anywhere from one day to two weeks).

**Families.com**
(http://www.families.com/become-a-blogger)

A Families.com Blogger is a paid professional writer who posts regularly on a given topic. A Families.com Blogger writes articles with a minimum of 300 words. Bloggers can blog for many different topics–as long as they have the expertise to write in that subject area.

A Families.com Blogger must be versatile, creative, experienced and well informed on their chosen topic. They must have a solid grasp of the English language and be able to edit their own work as well as take the direction of an editor.

Families.com is the blog network for family topics. We currently have more than 30 blogs on topics such as parenting, marriage, family fun, frugal living, and home & garden. Incomplete applications will not be considered, so please see below for exactly what should be included in your application package. Applications are accepted on an ongoing basis, however, we generally do not have immediate openings. When we have an opening, we look for the best qualified writer for the position.
What Do You Get by Writing for Families.com?

The opportunity to share your passion, to be published and to have your voice heard by large numbers of readers.
We take care of the technology, hosting, graphic design and marketing. There are no fees to you.

We will cross-promote your blog on Families.com.

We pay $4 per blog entry (There is a 90 day training period). We give annual raises, up to $5.50.

Bloggers are eligible for quarterly bonuses based on their performance.

What is Required of Families.com Bloggers?

» The Families.com blogs will only be as good as our bloggers. We are looking for amazing bloggers who can write passionate, high-quality, interesting, and thought-provoking articles.

» Some of our bloggers write 100+ posts per month while others only update their blog once or twice per week. How many posts you are able to write depends on the blog you are writing for. We do expect our bloggers to commit to their assignments and communicate with the editor should there be an issue in getting them done.

» Entries should be at least 300 words, but can be much longer. A post could include a tip or idea, a top 10 list, a story or quote, "how-tos", demos, photos, essays, or a product or entertainment review. The important thing is that whatever material you write is informative and/or entertaining for our readers.

» Review comments to your blog entries, delete inappropriate comments and respond to comments where appropriate.

Avoid topics that are not appropriate for the Families.com family-values centric audience, such as drug and alcohol abuse, profanity, gambling, pornography, extramarital sex, and nudity, except in the context of helping families to overcome these issues. There is definitely a place in the blogs for PG-rated discussions of intimacy and sexuality in marriage, however, these blogs are not the appropriate place for sensualized sexuality. Do not use the blog to advocate for a specific political party, religion, alternative lifestyle, abortion, etc. Please see us if you feel an exception needs to be made to this rule. It is appropriate to talk about faith and spirituality without advocating for a specific religion, or to talk about advocating for families without endorsing specific political candidates and parties.

» Successfully complete Families.com Blogger Training and a 90 day probationary period. Then, continue to maintain a high quality of blog posts and work well with the Families.com team.

We are looking for bloggers who are self-motivated, who have expertise in their topic, and who can add personality to their blog.

How Do I Apply to Be a Families.com Blogger?

» Select a Topic – Select 1 to 3 topics either from our list of current topics or topics you feel would add value to our community for which you would like to write. We do consider adding new blogs occasionally. PLEASE NOTE THE TOPIC(S) IN YOUR SUBJECT LINE.

» Samples – Please send two sample blogs. They should be related to your topics. If you have noted 3 topics, we still only need two samples. Samples should be at least 300 words long and give us a feel for your writing voice. Note: Please write an original sample related to your topic choice. We do not look at links in lieu of samples. (Additional information about the hiring process is on the website)

**Morningside Partners**
(http://www.flexjobs.com/jobs/telecommuting-jobs-at-morningside_partners_llc)

Morningside Partners LLC is the Washington, DC area company that produces verbatim transcripts of broadcast programming that appears on CNN, FOX News, MSNBC and CNBC, among other leading broadcast programs. Morningside also produces and distributes other select verbatim transcripts of corporate earnings and shareholder relations events and calls. Formed in 1993 under the name FDCH, Morningside has grown into a company with hundreds of employees and contractors dedicated to developing and publishing news for the electronic information marketplace. Morningside hires at-home transcribers to produce transcripts of live television programs on most of the major networks. In the past, Morningside has offered telecommuting jobs, full-time jobs, freelance jobs, and part-time jobs.

**Patch.com** (http://workathomemoms.about.com/gi/o.htm?zi=1/XJ&zTi=1&sdn=workathomemoms&cdn=parenting&tm=22&f=11&su=p284.13.342.ip_&tt=29&bt=3&bts=12&zu=http%3A//www.patch.com/jobs)
Online, local newspaper hiring several work-from-home positions. Must live in area where positions are available.

# FINANCE/ACCOUNTING AND BOOKKEEPING

**Book Minders** (http://www.bookminders.com/)
Accounting outsourcing firm hires home-based accountant and sales persons on a full- and part-time basis, offering benefits for some positions.

**Balance Your Books** (http://www.balanceyourbooks.com/jobs.shtml)
Accounting outsourcing firm hires CPAs, bookkeepers with experience providing A/P, A/R, payroll and general and sales people offering the "opportunity to telecommute."

**Bateman And Company** (http://www.batemanhouston.com/)
Accounting firm hires work-at-home accountants on a permanent, part-time basis. Texas residents preferred.

**Click Accounts** (http://www.clickaccounts.com/whowearecareers.html)
Business process outsourcing (BPO) service provider accepts resumes from accounting and bookkeeping professionals to work at home.


**E-Billing Solutions**
(http://e-billingsolutions.net/jobs/)

E-Billing Solutions is an equal opportunity employer. E-Billing Solutions has a "virtual" office, meaning each of our employees work from his/her home, determining their own hours. Employees must undergo a rigorous background check. Working knowledge of HIPAA is a prerequisite for employment.

E-Billing Solutions is always interested in adding qualified individuals for data entry, coding and receivables. Complete our online application below if you wish to be considered for any of these positions.


**First Data** (https://www.firstdata.com/en_us/home.html)
Transaction processing company hires management and sales professionals to work from home. Use "remote" in keyword field.

**VT Audit** (http://www.vtaudit.com/careers.asp)

Hires home-based auditors for workers' compensation and general liability audits for property and casualty insurance clients. Experience in processing payroll and working with bills of lading in shipping and receiving preferred. Special consideration given for applicants located in Kentucky, Michigan, Illinois, Nevada, Ohio, Massachusetts, Wisconsin and Colorado.

**Intuit** (http://www.intuitatwork2012.com/)
Industry:
Financial services and software
Company Description:
Based in Mountain View, CA, this financial software giant owns Quicken, QuickBooks, TurboTax, GoPayment, Mint.com and Intuit Healthcare Solutions. The company has 8,000 employees worldwide.

Types of Work-at-Home Opportunities at Intuit:
CPAs and enrolled agents can apply for Intuit jobs as work-at-home tax advisors for TurboTax
Intuit has a variety of remote positions in software engineering, sales, marketing and finance in the U.S. and Canada.

Qualifications, salaries and requirements will vary widely. However, its work-at-home, online tax advisor jobs, which support its TurboTax product, are a new part of its operations with the release of TurboTax 2011 and are in the U.S.

Online Tax Advisor Qualifications and Requirements:
These 500 to 1,000 tax advisor positions are for certified public accountants (CPA), enrolled agents (EA) and tax attorneys, who will support TurboTax products via phone, chat and email (with no required up selling) and provide written summaries of tax solutions to customers. Unlike a typical tax preparer job, these experts will give advice but won't actually do tax preparation.

Full- and part-time, seasonal positions are available. Some seasonal agents are promoted to permanent managerial positions. During tax season expect 30 to 40 hours per week of work. The season begins with paid training, which consists of training sessions taking place from November to January, and the season ends in late April. A variety of established schedules that cover the hours of 5 a.m. to 9 p.m. Pacific Time, seven days a week are available. However flexibility to take extra work during peak hours may be required.

Successful applicants for the online tax advisor must have active credentials as an enrolled agent or CPA and a preparer tax identification number (PTIN). Additionally tax advisors need a minimum of 5 years of experience preparing federal and state returns, extensive knowledge of tax laws, experience using tax preparation software, excellent verbal and written communication skills and the ability to work with minimal supervision and to research IRS and state publications, regulations, and GAAP publications. Bilingual ability and experience with electronic filing and software troubleshooting are considered a plus.
Advisors need a distraction-free space with a computer and phone and should be willing to commit to work 30 to 40 hours a week. Intuit has a made a point to promote these positions as military spouse jobs.

Pay and Benefits:
These tax advisor jobs are employment positions--not independent contractors--with benefits such as medical, dental, and 401K, as well as product discounts.
Intuit has not released the hourly salaries it will pay online tax advisors, but it says its agents who work the whole season can earn a bonus of $8,000. For context on the possible hourly wage, according to the Bureau of Labor Statistics, the average salary of a tax preparer is about $15.50 per hour. However, many tax preparers are not as experienced at Inuit's tax advisors and are not enrolled agents or CPAs, as required by Intuit. On the

other hand, work-at-home jobs sometimes pay less than their on-site counterparts.
Applying for Intuit Jobs:
Apply at Intuit jobs website. Use the keyword "remote" to find all the telecommuting jobs including the online tax advisor positions.

**OSI Business Services**
(http://www.flexjobs.com/jobs/telecommuting-jobs-at-osi_business_services)

OSI Business Services, LLC was started to provide an outsourced accounting department for small, mid-size and fast growing businesses. OSI dedicates a team of accounting professionals to each client, including a daily bookkeeper, an accounting software specialist, and a controller. Headquartered in Pompton Plains, New Jersey (NJ) provides work from home freedom with multiple remote opportunities in financial, bookkeeping and accounting roles. If you have a strong background in corporate finance and are seeking a rewarding telecommute option, then consider a job with OSI Business Services.

# INSURANCE

**Aetna**
(http://www.aetna.com/about-aetna-insurance/aetna-careers/working-at-aetna/why_flexible.html)

The company's careers website helps jobseekers find telecommuting jobs by allowing a specific search for potential telework positions. To search for telecommuting jobs at Aetna, first choose "Yes" in the drop-down menu under "Potential Telework Position." As mentioned above, these jobs only have the potential for telework in the future. To further refine these jobs to ones that are actually being hired as work-at-home jobs or to ones that have a definite plan to become telecommuting, use "telework" as your keyword. Next do a new search with "work at home" as a keyword as these will bring up different jobs.

This major insurance company hires nurses, physicians and managers to work from home. While some positions are specifically designed for telework, in others telework opportunities will be considered. Search jobs database with keyword "telework."

**ARO Contact Center** (http://www.callcenteroptions.com/shell.asp?p=hr)

Types of work at home insurance jobs: auditors
Though mostly a virtual call center, this BPO hires also has telecommuting jobs for insurance auditors--phone auditors and physical auditors. Both types of auditors conduct premium audits for general liability and workman's compensation, but the physical audits, though they complete most of audit by phone, include a final physical walk-through. Additionally, it has home-based positions for LPNs and RNs doing telehealth work. See more work-at-home jobs for LPNs.

Based in Kansas City, MO, ARO, Inc., utilizes an at-home workforce based inside the United States as it offers business process outsourcing (BPO) for companies in industries such as insurance, healthcare, pharmaceutical and energy.

Types of Work-at-Home Positions:
ARO hires only employees and not independent contractors. ARO offers both full- and part-time employees set schedules.
Some of the people ARO hires to service its clients include call center agents (customer services and B2B), insurance agents and auditors, and nurses (RN and LPN). More specifically, the positions for which it hires are:
Call center agents - Some positions are customer service only, e.g., medical history interviewers who take both inbound and outbound calls from applicants. These jobs require customer service skills, good listening and ability to document conversations using computer applications. Knowledge of medical terminology is a plus. Other call center jobs are for inbound and outbound sales. Experience in sales and a minimum commitment of 25 hours per week is required in these jobs.

Premium insurance auditor - Company hires both phone auditors and physical auditors. Phone auditors only use the phone and the computer to conduct premium audits for property and casualty insurance, i.e., general liability and workman's compensation. Physical auditors do the same but must do a final physical walk-through at the company being audited.

Licensed insurance agents - Company has work-at-home jobs for both life insurance and property and casualty agents making both inbound and outbound calls.

**Telehealth** – at ARO
Company hires nurses, both RNs and LPNs, for inbound and outbound calling positions.

Requirements:
While ARO hires in all U.S. states, it is not always hiring in every state. Applicants must have a dedicated work space with a door. No noise background noise from pets, children or other sources is tolerated. Also the agent must supply a computer, a high speed Internet (cable or DSL), a dedicated phone line with no call waiting features (VoIP services may be acceptable), and a basic telephone with amplifier and headset. Cordless and cell phones are not acceptable.

Applying to ARO:
To apply for any of these positions, go to ARO's website and click "Apply to Be a Remote Employee Today!" Fill out the contact information, choose which type of job for which you are applying and upload your resume. You should then receive a confirmation email. If the company is hiring in your area and you meet the requirements, you may receive another email inviting you to complete a full application and to interview by phone.

Training:
Training varies based on the position and can be done remotely or at a corporate location. Training is paid at the same as the regular hourly rate and lasts 6 to 10 weeks for 3 to 8 hours per day.

**Cigna** (http://careers.cigna.com/CIGNAPage.aspx?page=14)

Types of work at home insurance jobs: nurses (RN), providers relations analysts, contract managers, claims coordinators

Cigna hires several types of work at home insurance jobs including registered nurses to work-at-home as disability and workers comp clinical case managers. Try "work from home" and "work at home" as keywords to search Cigna's job openings.

**FARA** (https://yorkrsgcareers.silkroad.com/yorkext/EmploymentListings.html)

Types of work at home insurance jobs: auditors

Insurance services provider hires premium auditors, as independent contractors, for work at home positions. However, these insurance jobs require local travel.

**The Hartford**
(https://thehartford.taleo.net/careersection/2/moresearch.ftl?lang=en)
Types of work at home insurance jobs: nurses, adjusters, sales people, attorneys and claims consultants

Use the keyword "remote" to search the company's job listings...


**Humana** (https://www.humana.com/about/careers/)

Types of work at home insurance jobs: nurses (RN), medical coders, chart auditors, licensed insurance reps, accountants, physicians, writers and sales.

Headquartered in Louisville, Kentucky, Fortune 500 health insurance company Humana Inc. hires for several types of telecommuting positions. Choose "Work at Home" in the drop down menu in the company's job database for location.


**ING** (http://ing.us/about-ing/careers)
Types of work at home insurance jobs: underwriting, sales, marketing

Insurance and financial services company offers work at home positions in underwriting as well as home-based sales and marketing positions in both its insurance and investment management divisions.

**LiveOPs** (http://cloud.liveops.com/glp-liveops-multichannel-demo.html?gclid=CITD-8bxl7sCFbQWMgodTRkA1g)

Industry:
Call Center: at home insurance jobs: licensed insurance agents
Based in Santa Clara, CA, this privately held company provides call center outsourcing to clients using only U.S.-based home call center agents. Its more than 20,000 virtual call center agents are all independent contractors.

Types of Work at Home Opportunities:
Most calls are inbound sales calls; however there are several types of center agent positions:
Advanced sales agent - According to LiveOPs web page, the average advanced sales agent can invoice $9.62 per 30 minute block.

Outbound agents - According to LiveOPs web page, the average Outbound Agent makes $5.25 per 30 minute block but incentives are available.

Bilingual agents - French and Spanish
Roadside assistance agent -inbound/outbound sales, customer service and dispatch

Licensed insurance agent

Applying to Become a LiveOPs Agent:
LiveOPs agents are not employees but <u>independent contractors,</u> who are paid mostly on a per minute basis. Agents may schedule their time in blocks as short as 30 minutes. Agents must be 18 years old and reside in the 48 contiguous United States. LiveOPs does not charge a fee for training, but it does not pay during training. LiveOPs does charge a $50 fee to new agents for a background and credit check.
To apply to be a LiveOPs agent you must:
Create a login with a valid email address and sign in.
Provide information on your background, including information about sales experience.
Take an assessment for comprehension and computer skills (optional).
Verify that you understand the requirements.
Audition your voice.

Based in Santa Clara, CA, this privately held company provides call center outsourcing to clients using only U.S.-based home call center agents. Its more than 20,000 virtual call center agents are all independent contractors. Among the call center agents it hires are licensed insurance agents.


**MetLife** (https://www.metlife.com/careers/index.html?jobs=careers/job-search/sales-jobs/index.html)
Types of work at home insurance jobs: underwriters, analysts

Large insurance company hires underwriters and controls analysts for work from home positions. However, the company also has flexible workplace options (including telework) for other employees as well.

**Sedgwick Claims Management Service** (https://www.sedgwick.com/careers/Pages/default.aspx)

Types of work at home insurance jobs: claims service assistants
Claims management company with call centers in Michigan and Ohio hire claims service assistants either as work at home or with an eventual transition to working from home.

**United Health** (http://careers.unitedhealthgroup.com/)

Industry:
Insurance, Health Care

Types of work at home insurance jobs: nurses, contract managers, Medicaid specialists, auditors, analysts and consultants

Based in Minnetonka, Minnesota, health insurance company United Healthcare Group is a Fortune 500 company that offers telecommuting positions in nursing and other fields. More than 20 percent of this large health insurance company's employees take advantage of its telecommuting opportunities.
Company Description:
Based in Minnetonka, Minnesota, health insurance company UnitedHealthcareGroup is a Fortune 500 company (#21 in 2009) with 75,000 employees.

Types of Work-at-Home Positions:
More than 20 percent of this large health insurance company's employees take advantage of its telecommuting opportunities. UnitedHealth Group hires registered nurses for telecommuting positions as well as others with experience in the insurance industry. Many of the "work at home" nurse positions involve seeing patients in their homes but some are telephone-based positions.
Non-nursing positions that may be telecommute jobs include contract managers, Medicaid specialists, auditors, analysts, consultants and medical coders.
Using United Healthcare's Employment Page: UnitedHealth Group Website
Select "Yes" under the drop-down menu for "Telecommuter Positions" to find jobs eligible for telecommuting.


**Well Point** (http://wellpoint.jobs.net/all-jobs/?cbsid=6ea5584cd2fb4145bff91f2e703393ce-337422253-VN-4)

Types of work at home insurance jobs: insurance sales
One of the nation's largest health care companies, WellPoint allows some positions both in nursing and in other fields to be telecommuted after a certain amount of time in the office.

**Zurich in North America**
(http://www.zurichna.com/zna/careers/careers.htm)

Types of work at home insurance jobs: insurance sales, account executives
Search "work at home" in this insurance company's jobs database. Most remote positions are for account executives and occasionally an attorney.


**Parameds**
(http://www.wahadventures.com/2012/01/working-at-home-with-parameds.html)

Parameds is a work at home company.

Parameds, a company more than a decade old, is a third-party company who works to collect information for insurance companies. Parameds hires remote workers for the Attending Physician Statement Retriever position as well as roles like underwriting.
The Attending Physician Statement Retriever job does not require a lot of specific background or skills, which is why I have chosen to focus on this role.
What do Attending Physician Statement Retrievers (also referred to as APSs) do for Parameds?


Paramed APS workers make outbound calls to retrieve data on a case by case basis. It seems to most commonly involve calling medical offices to retrieve patient information on behalf of insurance companies. However, Parameds deals with more than just medical insurance. From disability and life insurance to death claims, there is a large market to be cared for by Paramed.

Equipment Requirements for the Attending Physician Statement Retrievers at Parameds?
You will need to download Skype to make your calls. Any fees when you use Skype for your calls are reimbursed by Parameds. Or, you have the choice of using your own home land line or even your cell phone but those charges are not covered by Parameds.
If you use Skype or any other VoIP service like Gmail's Calling Service, you will need to buy a USB headset that can be plugged into your computer. This expense is not covered by Parameds but is generally inexpensive.

You will also need a working space with a quiet background. You do not want to sound like you work at home by having sounds of your dog barking, TV blasting and kids talking in the background. A good noise canceling microphone and an office with a door with a lock makes for a nice working environment!

Is the Schedule at Parameds Flexible?
Oh this is the part about Parameds that I love! There is a lot of flexibility! You are required to be available for at least 6 hours a day Monday through Friday. However, as far as I have read, you are not given a set schedule of hours. Your 6 hours can be broken up throughout the day. There will be some 'cases' you will receive that will require you to call before 4:30pm in their time zone. Also, some of the supervisors like to see you start around the same time each day. But that is something you will discuss with your supervisor at the appropriate time.
While you are required to be available for at least 6 hours a day, it does not mean you will work 6 hours a day. Some days will require less and some may require more. This brings us to the next subject of discussion- how you are paid.

How Much does Parameds Pay their Work at Home APSs?
Parameds, like many other companies, keep their pay rate hidden under a privacy agreement signed before being hired. But it is important to know they do not pay on an hourly rate. A Very helpful forum posting said this about the Parameds pay:
You are paid per completed case which is dependable on how quickly you can close out your cases (your turnaround time). How long to complete is really dependable on the facility you work with and how well you can tempt them into rushing this for you. Some you can complete out within the 1st day of receiving the case and others could take 60+ days to complete.

What is the Pay Schedule at Parameds?
Parameds MAILS a check on the 1st and the 15th of each month. If payday is on a weekend or holiday, they will pay the next business day. Eeek. Parameds waits to pay out your first check until 30 days after you begin work! AND if you quit within that first 30 days, you forfeit your pay!!!

Parameds is simply not for everyone. It is a job that is filled with unknowns. You don't always know how much work you will have, how much your paycheck will be or if the next call you make will result in a screaming and attitude filled person you need to help you close out your case- so you can be paid for it!
So, How do you Apply for Parameds?
Send your resume to joinus@parameds.com  It is not always known if they are currently hiring, but sending an inquiry to Parameds is the best way to find out.

**Quest Diagnostics**
(http://jobs.heart.org/j/t-Teleinterviewer-I-PartTime-Work-From-Home-e-Quest-Diagnostics-Incorporated--l-Lees-Summit,-MO-jobs-j2721462.html)

At Quest Diagnostics Incorporated, we understand urgency. But more than speed, we focus our energies on accuracy. Currently, we seek a Part-Time Work at Home Teleinterviewer 1:
Responsibilities
Basic Purpose:
-This position completes life insurance applications via telephone for a single client company.

Training Hours:
-The Part-Time Work at Home Teleinterviewer 1 opportunity requires working from the ExamOne Lee's Summit, MO (800 NW Chipman Road Ste 5900; Lee's Summit, MO 64063) office for 6-8 weeks for training before working from home
-Training hours are Monday - Friday 5pm to 9pm

Work From Home Hours:
-Hours can vary, however, they are usually part-time evening hours

Required Equipment:
-DSL/Cable connection speed 1.0 Mbit down/256 Kb upload speed minimum
**(Cannot be through aWiFi internet connection or satellite provider)**
-Home telephone line with local Kansas City area number
**Note: the position requires the applicant to reside in the Kansas City metro area**
-Analog Phone
-Analog Headset
-Desk
-Chair
-Lighting
-Surge Protector
-Quiet Working Space
-The position may also require a router and multiple in home visits for setup and repair of equipment. The smart computer and all other necessary technical equipment will be provided by Quest Diagnostics

Principal Duties & Responsibilities:
-Complete interviews with life insurance applicants via telephone. These interviews will include gathering medical, financial, occupational, and avocation histories. Review and edit information collected during the interview for quality assurance purposes.

-Manage the C4 Call Management System by making telephone calls, logging call attempts, documenting information within orders as necessary and recording call results.
-Responds to the needs and requests of clients and Quest Diagnostics management and staff in a professional and expedient manner.
-Observes all compliance policies and safety policies and procedures as outlined in the Quest Diagnostics
-Safety Manual or safety matters included in other special training

Knowledge & Experience:
-High School Diploma or Equivalent required, some college courses preferred.

Minimum Skills Required:
-Ability to type 25 wpm adjusted for accuracy
-Strong communication skills
-Accurate, detail oriented
-Proficient teamwork skills
-Good work attendance record
-Organizational skills
-Six (6) Months Customer service experience

Minimum Skills Preferred:
* Background in Medical Terminology

Want to be able to wear your fuzzy slippers to work? How about save over $1,800 on fuel expenses? Our Part-Time Work at Home Teleinterviewer 1 do both!
How To Apply
Please Log In or Register to Upload a Resume and complete the online Application. Because of the large number of applicants to job openings, Quest Diagnostics will only contact candidates to be interviewed.

*Live every moment*
*Love beyond words*
*Laugh everyday*

# MEDIA AND ARTS

**Avanti Press** (http://www.avantipress.com/#/about/)
Photography, Writing
Pet-centric greeting card maker licenses photographs from freelancers. Occasionally accepts new verse writers

**BC Virtual Tour** (http://www.bcvirtualtour.com/opportunities.html)
Take pictures of homes on the real estate market in British Columbia for a commission and travel expenses.

**The Bradford Group** (http://www.thebradfordgroup.com/careers/)
Designers, Illustrators
Collectibles Company seeks freelance artists to work with its product Development teams
On products that include collector plates from The Bradford Exchange, ornaments and music boxes from Bradford Editions, cottages from Hawthorne Village, and figurines from The Hamilton Collection.

**Cape Shore**
(http://www.cape-shore.com/?page_id=13&PHPSESSID=2c807034f7802145d86cf404427f765e)
Artists/Illustrators
Company hires freelance artists working in acrylic, gouache, watercolor, oil paint, pastel and mixed media collage to create work in a variety of themes (nautical, Christmas, regional, floral, etc.) for its line of paper products.

**Cricket Magazine** (http://www.cricketmag.com/17-Illustration-Guidelines-for-Cobblestone-Publishing-Companys-six-magazines-for-kids-ages-6-and-up)

Illustrators
A magazine accepts hand-drawn and computer-generated illustrations from freelancers.
Send non-returnable samples for consideration for an assignment.

**Demand Studios** (http://create.demandstudios.com/)

Video Producers, Writers
Demand Studios accepts applicants with writing, editing and filmmaking skills.
They are assigned to produce made-for-the-Internet content that appear on sites like eHow.com, LIVESTRONG.COM and dozens more sites. Writers are paid both on a flat fee and revenue sharing basis.

**Driver Guide**
(http://www.flexjobs.com/jobs/telecommuting-jobs-at-driverguide.com)

Driver Guide is an award winning database of thousands of product software drivers, firmware and support documents (manuals) for hundreds of technology products available on the current and past markets. Often hard to find drivers for computer peripherals can be found on Driver Guide thanks to their tireless search and the talents of their IT team. The company continues to experience growth and therefore has multiple opportunities to work from home as a database helper, PHP Developer or Graphic Designer. These positions are part time, with some degree of flexibility available. Training is provided to qualified candidates who are then allowed to work from the comfort of their home as virtual professionals. To find out more about the telecommuting opportunities that Driver Guide can offer you, be sure to check out the links on Flex jobs.

**Excel Sportswear** (http://exceltees.com/careers/artists/)
Illustrators, Cartoonists
Sportswear Company hires freelancers to supplement its in-house art staff in creating original illustrations of mascots, cars and high school sports.

**Look Better Online** (http://www.lookbetteronline.com/)
Photographers
Portrait photographers take pictures of clients who need images for dating sites. Home studios are OK, if they meet certain requirements.

**Marion Health** (http://www.marianheath.com/)
*Artists/Illustrators*
Greeting Card company accepts submissions for everyday greetings for some humor.

**Metaphor Studios** (http://www.metaphor-studio.com/)

Writers, Graphic Designers, Illustrators, Marketing Professionals, and Web Designers Metaphor Studio are a creative consultancy that specializes in building brand communities.
Two years experience required.

**Nature Friend**
(http://www.naturefriendmagazine.com/index.pl?linkid=11;class=gen)
*Photography*
Monthly magazine purchases nature photography freelancers.

**Oatmeal Studios**
(http://www.oatmealstudios.com/Artist%27sGuidelines/AG-Pg.htm)

*Artists, Cartoonist*
Artist's guidelines for greeting card company call for "fresh and fun-looking artwork in any media and style. Also, sophisticated, funky cartoony-type art (people and/or animals) with or without words. Color work is best."

**Obeo** (http://www.obeo.com/public/global/jobopportunities.aspx)
*Photographers*
Take pictures of homes on the real estate market. Amateurs accepted. Freelance photographers are at the core of our business. We are looking for people with a photography background (amateur or professional) or for those who wish to be in the photography industry and have their own equipment. At Obeo we require external flash photography on all of our homes, so you need a little more than just a digital camera.
Photography orders are forwarded to you via e-mail and it will be your responsibility to:
Set appointments
Photograph the home
Process and upload photos to our website
It normally takes less than 30 min to photograph a home and less than 20 min to process the photos for each home. Payment is on a "per house" basis for each property that you photograph as a sub-contractor.
 Payment amounts depend on what type of photography is requested and the general market conditions in which you live.

**Opuzz Voice**
(http://www.opuzz.com/voice_submission.asp)
Voice actors doing recordings from home. They are not accepting submissions at the time this book is published. Be ready for when they do.

**Papryus**
(http://www.papyrusonline.com/category/about+papyrus/artist+submission+guidelines.do)
*Artists, Illustrators, Photographers*

Greeting card and stationary company purchases from freelance artists a range of materials from graphics, traditional, whimsical, humor and contemporary pieces to photography.

**Recycled Paper Greeting** (http://www.prgreetings.com/)
*Artists*
Freelance artists can submit artwork along with a message for consideration for Greeting Card Company.
Does not accept electronic submissions.


**The Sun Magazine**
(http://thesunmagazine.org/about/submission_guidelines/writing)

*Writers, Photographers* Pay ranges for freelance writing assignments (essays, interviews, fiction and poetry) from $300 to $2,000. One-time use of photos pays $100-$500.

> Be Remarkable.
> Be Generous.
> Create Art.
> Make Decisions.
> Make Connections.

# MEDICAL TRANSCRIPTION

**Accentus** (http://www.accentusinc.com/careers/us.php)

Industry:
Medical document management firm, i.e., medical BPO specializing in transcription and medical coding.
Company hires experienced work-at-home medical transcriptionists for a variety of shifts as well as coders.

Company Description:
Accentus, which was formerly called Transolutions and is now part of Nuance Healthcare, is headquartered in Ottawa, Ontario, but it offers services hires in both the United States and Canada. The company offers medical transcription services to doctors, clinics and hospitals and medical coding to his hospital clients.

Types of Work-at-Home Opportunities at Accentus:
The company offers remote medical transcription jobs in the U.S. and Canada. In the U.S. some of these positions (acute division) are for employees, while the jobs in the U.S. ambulatory division and the Canadian jobs in both ambulatory and acute are for independent contractors.
In medical coding, it hires experienced, certified medical coders and coding quality assurance staff. These opportunities are for work-at-home and on-site (travel-to-client) coders.

More on these types of positions:
A medical transcriptionist practices a specialized form of transcription. He or she listen to a physician or medical practitioner's dictated notes regarding a patient and transcribes them for addition into the patient's medical file.
Typically a medical transcriptionist uses similar. Medical coding jobs can often be done from home. However, certification and experience (typically about three years) are usually required for work-at-home, medical coding jobs.

Requirements for Medical Transcription Jobs:
In the United States:
The acute division, which serves hospitals and multi-specialty clinics, hires part-time employees for 24-32 hours per week's week for shifts cover all hours in the day. Weekend work is required. One year of acute care transcription/editing experience is required.

Additionally experience on accounts with 40+ dictators and ESL dictators are needed. Windows-based computer with XP or Windows 7 is required. These jobs offer medical/dental insurance, paid time off, Internet reimbursement and other benefits. The ambulatory division hires experienced, independent contractors for flexible schedules of mostly weekdays.

These jobs do not offer benefits.

In Canada
Both the ambulatory and acute division positions are for independent contractors only. In the acute division,
transcriptionists should be certified or have two years training and a minimum of two years recent experience transcribing and editing in acute care. However, the recent completion of an accredited medical transcription course with an average of 90 percent or higher may be substituted for experience.
Transcribers must commit to produce a minimum of 250-300 audio minutes per week
 (approximately 20-25 hours).
In the ambulatory division, most of the jobs are full-time contract positions for transcriptionists with a minimum of 3- to 5-years experience within a specific specialty that can produce 80 audio minutes per day. Hours are typically weekdays.

Requirements for Medical Coding Jobs:
Coders in the U.S. must have certification, such as CCS or CCS-P and/or CPC or CPC-H, RHIT and RHIA, as well as 3- to 5-years coding experience. Those applying to remote coding positions should have experience working in a virtual office. (On-site coders must be available to travel.)

Applying to Accentus:
Choose either the Acctentus Career Canada page or Accentus Careers United States.

Then choose the type of work--coding or transcription--and apply through its online applications system.

**Applied Medical Services** (http://www.fastchart.com/about/careers/)
Company hires independent contractors in as home-based medical transcription jobs as well as for medical billing and coding jobs.

**Eight Crossing** (http://www.eightcrossings.com/career.php)
Sacramento-based Eight Crossings recruits for medical transcription jobs in its office and for working at home. Two years experience required.

**Medifax Inc.** (http://nhwaa.com/jobsd-1128-.html)

Virtual Transcription and Data Entry Jobs at Medifax inc.

Careers are available in multiple arenas in this exciting, fast-paced, and rapidly growing organization. We are seeking US-based medical transcriptionists with a minimum of two years of experience in medical transcription or Certification in lieu of experience.

Due to the stat nature of the business, we are open 24 hours a day, 365 days a year. Employees are requested to work every other weekend or the equivalent of 32 hours of weekend time per month.

Both in-office and remote positions are available. Career advancement opportunities - including 3 levels for MTs, trainers, supervisors and quality assurance specialists - are available. For more information, please contact us.

Requirements:

VOIP/PBX System
eFAX System
Virtual Resume
Resume
Recent Graduate from an approved Transcription program

**Medi Grafix**
(http://www.flexjobs.com/jobs/telecommuting-jobs-at-medigrafix)

Based in Central Nebraska, Medigrafix is a medical transcription service serving the needs of hospitals, clinics, outpatient departments and physicians. Since 1986, MediGrafix has been the leading medical transcription service in the Midwestern United States. Utilizing existing technology, as well as keeping pace with new and developmental hardware and software, MediGrafix has been providing experienced professional medical transcription service to leading hospitals and clinics across the country. The workforce behind Medigrafix is comprised of many work from home healthcare information specialists who work in full and part time flexible telecommuting assignments.

**Med Quist**
(http://www.flexjobs.com/jobs/telecommuting-jobs-at-medquist)

Since 1970, when MedQuist was started, the company has been a leader in medical transcription services. As one of the first to develop computer-based medical transcription MedQuist now offers their transcription software technology services to an over 1,500 organizations throughout the United States. The services provided by MedQuist are digital voice capture, speech recognition, electronic signature, medical coding systems and services, and mobile dictation devices. MedQuist is one of largest employers of medical transcriptionist in the United States transcribing over 1.5 billion lines of text each year. Currently, MedQuist employs over

7,500 employees in a variety of job functions. Employees of MedQuist receive health insurance, paid time off, retirement savings plans, and disability insurance. The transcriptionists that work for MedQuist enjoy working out of their home offices either part-time or full-time with flexible work schedules.


**M*Model** (http://mmodal.com/about-us/careers/)

M*Modal telecommute jobs include professional, transcription, coding and support positions. Transcriptionists must have one Year of recent work experience as a medical transcriptionist or must be a recent graduate of an AAMT certified transcription program.

**Mountain West Processing**
(http://www.flexjobs.com/jobs/telecommuting-jobs-at-mountain_west_processing)

Mountain West Processing is a division of the Mountain West Communications company that researches and provides professional medical coding, transcription and corporate research services to a variety of medical, bio-research, technology and pharmaceutical companies. Work from home jobs with Mountain West Processing include medical and general business transcription. If you are an experienced transcriptionist and want the freedom to work at home, come work for one of the top paying companies in the US.

**M Record**
(http://careers.mrecord.com/transcribers_job_application.aspx)

MRecord Outsourced Business Services Group (MOBSG) is hiring At-home Medical Document Specialists (also known as Medical Transcriptionist). This position is STRICTLY ONLY available to Residents of the US who are legally authorized to work in the US.

You must be an active Medical Transcriptionist within the last five years. possess a minimum of six months' transcription experience,
be a legal resident of the continental United States with valid work authorization.

Other healthcare experience, (medical secretary, R.N., M.D.) does not apply toward the transcriptionist experience requirement.
Other transcription experience (court reporter, administrative assistant, MT for insurance workers' compensation) also does not apply.

The application is a three step process.

**NetMed Transcription**
(http://www.netmedtranscription.com/Employment.html)

If you're interested in working with NetMed Transcription Services or would like additional information about the company, please email Tami Gregg at tgregg@netmedtranscription.com.

Or send your resume to:
NetMed Transcription Services, L.L.C.
2604 Sunnyside Drive
Cadillac, MI 49601
ph 1.800.981.6676

**Nuance** (http://www.nuance-nts.com/default.asp)
Medical documentation services company, formerly known as Webmedx, hires medical transcriptionists and quality assurance specialists.

**Professional Medical Services**
(http://www.professionalmedicalservices.org/mt_requirements.html)
Hires medical transcriptionists with at least 4 years of experience in hospital transcription for acute care accounts. Part-time and full-time positions are for independent contractors.

**Portal Healthcare Solutions/Ascend**
(http://www.ascendhealthcare.com/Contact_Employment.html)
Company has opportunities for medical transcriptionists and quality assurance specialists as well as sales and operations.

**Spectra Medi**
(http://www.flexjobs.com/jobs/telecommuting-jobs-at-spectrum_health)

Spectrum Health offers a wide range of healthcare services to individuals in communities throughout the state of Michigan with headquarters in Grand Rapids, Michigan. Spectrum Health is a not-for-profit healthcare system that provides services for its patients through a variety of facilities that includes a medical center, community hospitals, a children's hospital, medical groups, physician groups, and its own health plan. Spectrum Health has been the recipient of numerous awards including the "101 Best and Brightest Companies to Work For" and Thomson Reuters' "Top 10 Health Systems in the Nation." In addition, Spectrum Health is one of the largest employers in Michigan with over 21,000 staff and physician employees and a network of more than 2,000 volunteers. With its network of facilities, Spectrum Health typically offers a variety of employment opportunities to start or continue a career in the healthcare industry

**Spheris**
(http://www.flexjobs.com/jobs/telecommuting-jobs-at-spheris)

Spheris is a leading global provider of clinical healthcare information documentation technology and services to more than 500 healthcare providers, hospitals and group practices throughout the U.S. Founded by doctors to aid them with their medical documentation needs, Spheris solutions address the needs of practitioners, health information directors, IT directors and administrators. Their intimate understanding of how doctors and healthcare facilities work enables them to combine advanced technology with expert remote teams to deliver comprehensive solutions. Spheris employs approximately 5,500 skilled medical language specialists, who work from home supporting the company's clients through a secure network. If you are a medical transcriptionist looking for a great place to call home and enjoy a telecommuting job, then consider working for Spheris.

**Ubiqus**
(http://www.ubiqus.com/GB/recruitment.htm)

Ubiqus is an Equal Opportunity Employer. It considers all positions without regard to race, religion, color, sex, national origin, age, disability or other categories as proscribed by federal, state or local law.

Fill out our online application. If we are interested in your credentials, we will contact you by email or telephone:

Note: Transcriptionist Applicants, please read our disclaimer before beginning your application

Verbatim Transcriptionist

Medical Transcriptionist

Summary Writer

Medical Summary Writer

Translator

Interpreter

Foreign Language Transcriptionist

Audio Technician

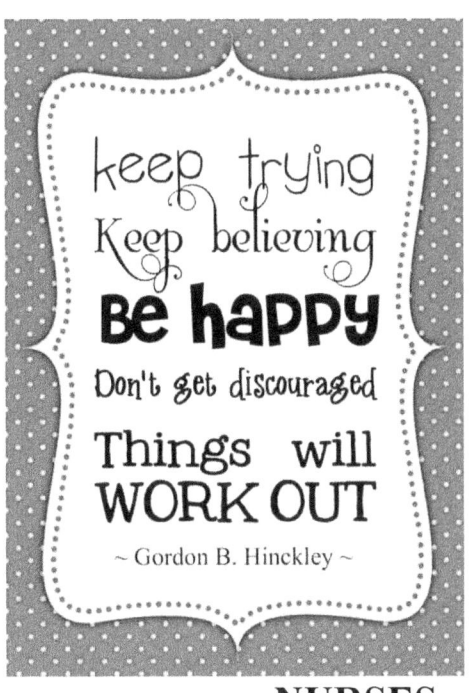

# NURSES

**About.com Health Channel** (http://www.about.com/health/)

Medical work-at-home jobs include: Nurses, physicians, medical writers
About.com contracts with more than 1,000 guides and topic writers who are experts in their many different fields including many medical professions. Pay starts at $675 per month but compensation increases with page view growth. Nurses and physicians are often hired in the Health Channel.

**Aetna**
(http://www.aetna.com/about-aetna-insurance/aetna-careers/)

Medical work-at-home jobs include: Nurses and physicians are among the Medical Professions who work from home at the insurance company.

**American International Group** (AIG)
(http://www.aig.com/careers_3171_437777.html )

Medical work-at-home jobs include: Nurses
After a specific amount of time working on-site, this company allows some nursing positions, such as case managers and medical reviewers to be telecommuted. Try keywords "telecommuting" or "work-from-home" in jobs database.

**ARO** (http://www.aroptions.com/about-us/careers.php)
While most of the home-based jobs at this BPO are for customer service, sales and 2B telemarketing agents, it also serves patients with nurse's telehealth.

**Carenet** (https://www.care-net.org/aboutus/employment.php)

Medical work-at-home jobs include: Nurses
Based in San Antonio, this medical Business Process Outsourcing (BPO) provides support to insurance Companies and health care systems. Virtual call center agents who are registered nurses (RNs) answer Questions or perform telephone triage. Pay sis $25 per hour.
Industry:
Health Care, Medical Call Center
Company Description:
Headquartered in San Antonio, Texas, Carenet is health care services company that offers its clients—which include employers, insurance companies, hospitals and other medical providers, and government--the services of a medical call center staffed by registered nurses working from home.

Types of Work-at-Home Positions:
For its work-at-home jobs, Carenet hires registered nurses as "Care Advisors." (It does have customer service call center jobs for non-nurses, but these are not work-at-home jobs.) The types of services these RNs provide include telephone triage, medical decision support, medical device monitoring services, member engagement and health care support. This is a 24-hour service, so overnight shifts may be available and/or required.

Requirements and Qualifications:
Successful applicants must have a two-year nursing degree at minimum, an unrestricted, current Texas RN license (or a current state license as a RN with the ability to become licensed in Texas), three years of clinical experience in acute, ambulatory area or telehealth. Carenet hires in Nurse Licensure Compact (NCL) states in the U.S. Currently these include Colorado, Iowa, Maryland, Mississippi, Missouri, Nebraska, New Hampshire, North Carolina, South Carolina, South Dakota, Tennessee, Texas, Virginia, Wisconsin. Onsite training in Texas may be required.

Compensation and Benefits:
Pay is approximately $25 per hour*. Employees receive options for medical, dental, vision insurance, 401(k), life insurance, paid time off and holidays.
Using Carenet's Employment Page: Carenet Employment website

Click on above link then choose "Clinical Services (RN)." Choose Care Advisor, and then follow the link to submit an online application.

**Cigna**  (http://careers.cigna.com/)

Industry:
Insurance, Healthcare

Company Description:
Cigna Corporation is a global health insurance and services company with more than 30,000 employees worldwide. Based in Bloomfield, CT, it was formed in 1982 with the merger of the Connecticut General Corporation and INA Corporation.

The company offers health insurance and a variety related products and services such as medical, dental and supplemental insurance; behavioral health, pharmacy and vision care; benefits management; health coaching; condition management; and group life, accident and disability insurance. Cigna is named one of my as one of my top major corporations for telecommuting.

In 2002 the company began a pilot work-at-home employment program mostly aimed at claims workers and field health care workers. Today more than 3,000 workers telecommute.[*] On the company's website it touts its "results-driven environment." Such environments are usually conducive to telecommuting.

Types of Work at Home Opportunities:
Cigna hires several types of work at home jobs including registered nurses to work-at-home as disability and workers comp clinical case managers as well as data and providers-relations analysts, contract managers and claims coordinators.

Pay and Benefits:
Pay varies with position.
Cigna offers a number of benefits for full-time employees, which include health, dental, vision, life and long-term care insurance; educational assistance, elder, adoption and child care assistance, flexible work arrangements and 401(k).

The company's jobs database has no specific selection for finding telecommuting jobs postings.
Use the keyword field to narrow the search. Try both "work from home" and "work at home" as keywords to search job openings.
Insurance company Cigna's division Intracorp hires RNs to work at home as disability and workers' comp Case manager. Use "work from home" as keywords to search Cigna's job openings. Hiring is done from a NY location.

**Conifer Health Solutions** (http://coniferhealth.com/careers/)
Medical work-at-home jobs include: Nurses, Medical coding

**Covance** (http://jobsearch.covance.com/)

This U.S.-based biopharmaceutical development services company, or a contract research organization, or a contract research organization, has preclinical and clinical research operations in more than 25 Countries and more than 10,000 employees worldwide. It hires clinical research associates to work from home and physicians as medical directors in specific locations in the U.S., Canada and Europe.
Use "home-based" to search its jobs database.

**Fonemed** (http://fonemed.com/employment)

Medical work-at-home jobs include: Nurses Company hires registered nurses from the United States and Canada to work from home to provide Telephone triage and health care advice to callers from
across North America. Also hires on-site customer Service reps, based in Newfoundland, Canada; need a minimum of a high school diploma.

**After-Hrs Triage** (www.intellatriage.com)
RN Based triage Service for Hospice and Home Health – IntellaTriage

**The Hartford**
(https://thehartford.taleo.net/careersection/2/moresearch.ftl?lang=en)
Medical work-at-home jobs include: Nurses
Type "remote" in the address for at-home positions.


**Healthfirst**
(https://re13.ultipro.com/HFM1000/JobBoard/SearchJobs.aspx?Page=Search)
Medical work-at-home jobs include: Nurses New York based health insurance company hires nurses as case managers to work from home.

**Health Net** (http://careersathealthnet.com/)
Medical work-at-home jobs include: Nurses
Health insurance company operating in 27 states hire nurses as case managers, care coordinators and care Managers with the option to telecommute. Use "telecommuting" as search keyword of company's job database.

**Humana** (https://www.humana.com/about/careers/)
Types of work at home insurance jobs: nurses (RN), medical coders, chart auditors, licensed insurance reps, accountants, physicians, writers and sales.

**Inland Empire Health Plan** (https://ww3.iehp.org/en/about-iehp/careers/)
Medical work-at-home jobs include: Nurses
The nation's largest health care services company, McKesson specializes in pharmaceutical distribution and health care IT systems and software.

**Nursing Home Telehealth** (www.completetelehealthsolution.com)
Patient monitoring system designed for nursing homes communities.

**Nemours** (http://careers.nemours.org/)
Pediatric health system with locations in Delaware, New Jersey, Pennsylvania, Washington, DC, and Florida hires work from home telephone triage nurses.

**Indeed.com** Telecommuting Nurse Jobs
Search current job postings for telecommuting nurse.

**Nurse Telephone Triage** (http://www.nursetriage.org/)
Medical work-at-home jobs include: Nurses
Company hires RNs with five years of nursing experience (preferably in pediatrics), telephone Triage experience and knowledge of and experience in using Barton Schmitt protocols.

**Paradigm Health Services**
(http://www.paradigmhealth.org/General%20Pages/Employment%20Pages/employment%20opportunities.htm)
Medical work-at-home jobs include: Nurses
Company hires licensed nursing professionals in Tennessee, Mississippi, North Carolina, Virginia, Kentucky and Georgia for full and part-time positions. Some telehealth positions available.

**Pathway Medical Staffing** (http://www.pathway-medical.com/)
Medical work-at-home jobs include: Nurses
Medical recruiting firm, in the New York City metro area
Specializes in non-clinical nursing positions.
Search using keyword "telecommute."

**PPD** (http://www.ppdi.com/Careers.aspx)
Medical work-at-home jobs include: Clinical research associates (BS in science field or RN certification required), medical writers This global contract research organization (CRO) provides drug discovery,

development and life-cycle management services within the health care industry.
It hires medical writers and clinical research associates (CRA) for work-at-home positions.

**Professional Dynamics**
(http://www.pdimcs.com/professional-dynamics-careers.aspx)
Medical work-at-home jobs include: Nurses, physicians
California-based company provides service in the workers compensation industry and to first party medical and employee benefit sectors. Some nurse case manager and physician peer review positions are telecommuting.

**Remote Medical International**
(http://www.remotemedical.com/About-Us/employment)

Medical work-at-home jobs include: Nurses, physicians
The "remote" in the name of Seattle-area Company refers to faraway places not working at home.
However, the company does have a telemedicine department and some other telecommuting jobs.

**SironaHealth** (http://www.sironahealth.com/careers)
Medical work-at-home jobs include: Nurses

**Triage 4 Pediatrics**
(http://www.triage4pediatrics.com/employment.shtml)
Medical work-at-home jobs include: Nurses
Based in Plano Texas this company hires RNs in the DFW are to work at home in after hours telephone triage. Requirements include 3-5 years in pediatrics, licensure in Texas, carrying malpractice insurance and drug test. Weekends and evenings are required but part-and full-time schedules are available.

**United Health Group** (http://careers.unitedhealthgroup.com/)

Medical work-at-home jobs include: Nurses, LPNs, medical coders
More than 20 percent of this large health insurance company's employees take advantage of its telecommuting opportunities. UnitedHealth Group hires registered nurses for telecommuting positions as well as others with experience in the insurance industry.

**WellPoint**
(http://wellpoint.jobs.net/AllJobs/?cbsid=6ea5584cd2fb4145bff91f2e703393ce-337422253-VN-4)

Medical work-at-home jobs include: Nurses
One of the nation's largest health care companies, WellPoint allows some positions, in nursing and in other fields, to be telecommuted after a certain amount of time in the office.

# MEDICAL CODING

**Accentus** (http://www.accentusinc.com/careers/us.php)

Company, formerly known as Transolutions, hires as employees experienced work-at-home medical transcriptionists for a variety of shifts as well as medical coders in the U.S. and Canada.
Requires Certification as a CCS or CCS-P and/or as a CPC or CPC-H but RHIT and RHIA credentials will qualify as well.
Company hires RHIA, RHIT, CCA-P, CPC, CPC-H, or CCS with at least three years of recent multi-specialty coding experience for full-time and part-time positions.

**Amphion Medical Services**
(http://amphionmedical.com/careers/coders-coding-reviewers/)
Company hires RHIA, RHIT, CCA-P, CPC, CPC-H, or CCS with at least three years of recent multi-specialty coding experience for full-time and part-time positions.

**Aviacode** (http://www.aviacode.com/coders/working-at-aviacode-faq)
Hires independent-contractor medical coders with three years of coding experience and at least one certification from either AAPC or AHIMA. According to its website, coders
could earn from $18-$30 per hour. Managers and quality assurance supervisors are employees often hired from the ranks of its independent contractors.

**The Coding Network, LLC**
(http://www.codingnetwork.com/medical-coding-jobs/)
Medical coders must have three years of coding experience in a particular clinical specialty and certification by one of the industry's credentialing bodies (AHIMA, AAPC, RCCB, ACMCS, etc).

**Conifer Health Solutions** (http://coniferhealth.com/careers/)

Health care services firm that focuses on the financial and patient communication aspects of health care hires work from home employees in nursing and coding as well as sales.
AHIMA certification and three years of experience required. Use "telecommuting" as a keyword to find home-based positions.

**Humana** (https://www.humana.com/about/careers/)

Many of this major health care company's work-at-home positions have geographic requirements. Its medical coding jobs from home require coding certification (RHIT, RHIA, or CCS) and may require travel to its Louisville, KY headquarters. In addition to medical coding jobs from home it hires RN positions are for field healthcare and involve visiting patients at home. It also sometimes has opportunities for registered nurses, chart auditors, licensed insurance reps, accountants, physicians, writers and sales people for remote positions.

**Maxim Health Information Services** (http://www.maximhealthinformationservices.com/remote-medical-coding-jobs.aspx)

A subsidiary of Maxim Healthcare Services, a healthcare staffing company, MHIS provides medical coding, auditing, and clinical documentation improvement services to clients.
It offers both on-site and remote medical coding jobs.

**Precyse** (http://careers.precyse.com/(X(1)S(aiezulrorat5tmzezzmwe4wz))/default.aspx?AspxAutoDetectCookieSupport=1)

Healthcare information management outsourcing company hired medical coders, transcriptionists, quality assurance specialists, registrars and auditors to work from home. Choose "All Remote
Locations" for location in its jobs database. Coders must have active RHIA, RHIT, CCS, CCS-P, CPC or CPC-H certification and a minimum of three years' experience coding inpatient records in a hospital HIM department.

**Pyramid Healthcare Solutions** (http://www.pyramidhs.com/healthcare-consultant-careers.html)
In addition to remote jobs for medical coders, this company also offers work at home jobs for coding managers, auditors and sales persons. Check "Nationwide Remote" for location in the jobs database.

**United Health Group** (http://careers.unitedhealthgroup.com/)
Search United Health Group's jobs database with the keyword "coder" and the "Telecommute" drop-down menu to "Yes."

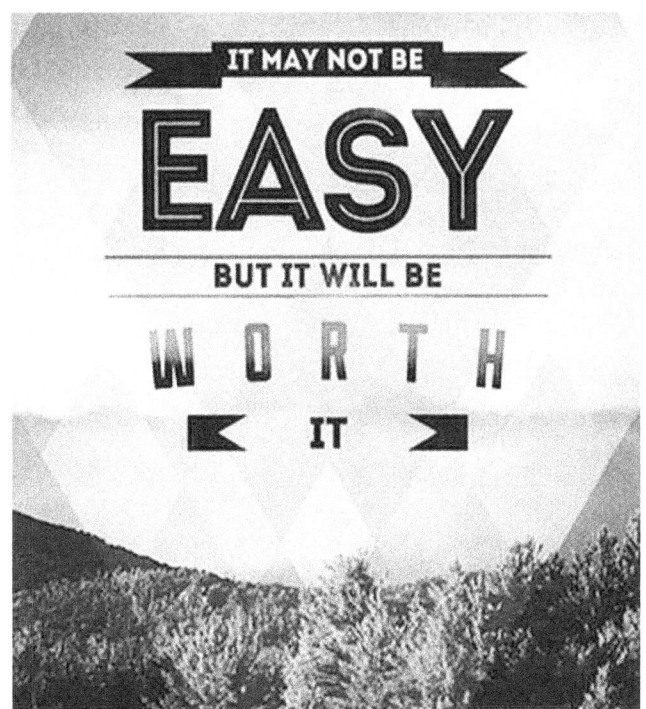

# MEDICAL CALL CENTER

**Aetna** (http://www.aetna.com/about-aetna-insurance/aetna-careers/find-a-career/)

Major insurance company offers telephone jobs for nurses, mental health professionals, and CSRs that are listed as "potential telework" positions. Unless the job posting specifically
says it will hire telecommuters, this likely means that telecommuting will be considered for an employee after a certain amount of time--perhaps a year.

**ARO** (http://www.callcenteroptions.com/shell.asp?p=hr)

While most of the home-based jobs at this BPO are for general customer service, sales and B2B telemarketing agents, it also has virtual positions for LPNs and RNs doing telehealth call center work as well as jobs for insurance auditors.

**Carenet**
(http://workathomemoms.about.com/od/medicalandnursingjob1/p/Carenet.htm)

Texas-based firm provides support to insurance companies and health care systems across the country. Its home-based medical call center of registered nurses (RN) answer questions
or perform telephone triage. It hires CS in San Antonio, but these are not work-at-home positions.

**Fonemed** (http://www.flexjobs.com/jobs/telecommuting-jobs-at-fonemed)

Company hires registered nurses from the United States and Canada to work from home to provide telephone triage and health advice to callers from across North America. Also hires customer service reps that need a minimum of a high school diploma.

**The Hartford**
(http://www.careerbuilder.com/Jobs/Company/C8F1336GLZ3MC7LND99/The-Hartford/)
In addition to hiring RNs for remote telephone jobs as case managers, this insurance company hires others in non-medical WAH jobs, such as claims representatives. Check off the option for remote jobs in the company's job listings.

**Health Net** (http://careersathealthnet.com/)
Heath insurance company operating in 27 states hires nurses as case managers, care coordinators and care managers with the option to telecommute. While not exactly call center jobs, the care manager jobs have a significant amount of telephone contact with patients. Use "telecommuting "as a search keyword of company's job database.

**Humana** (https://www.humana.com/about/careers/)
The telephonic nursing jobs at Humana go beyond the basics of medical call centers (such as telephone triage) into field such as case management and quality assurance, but many of them list call center experience as a requirement. Some of its work-at-home positions have geographic requirements. Check off "Virtual/Work at Home" in the company's jobs database.

**Medical Services Bureau**
(http://www.medicalservicebureau.com/Jobs/Index.htm)
After on-site training in El Paso, TX, or Austin, TX, part-time medical call processors can work from home. The job duties include for answering inbound calls, taking short messages and confirming information.

**Nurse Telephone Triage Service**
(http://www.nursetriage.org/nowhiring.html)
Company hires RNs with five years nursing experience (preferably in pediatrics), telephone triage experience and knowledge of and experience in using Barton Schmitt protocols.


**SironaHealth**
(http://www.sironahealth.com/about-us/careers/open-positions)
Company hires nurse consultants (RNs) to practice telephone triage or computer-assisted nursing through Inbound and outbound telephone calls with patients whose physicians, hospitals, insurers or employers are SironaHealth clients. Company has customer service rep (CSR) and medical service rep (MSR) positions for non-nurses but these jobs are based in Maine.

**Triage 4 Pediatrics**
(http://www.triage4pediatrics.com/employment.shtml)

Based in Plano, TX, this company hires RNs in the DFW area to work at home in after-hours Telephone triage. Requirements include 3-5 years in pediatrics, licensure in Texas, carrying malpractice insurance and drug test. Weekends and evenings are required but part- and full-time schedules are available.

**UnitedHealth** (http://careers.unitedhealthgroup.com/search-jobs.aspx)

More than 20 percent of this large health insurance company's employees take advantage of its telecommuting opportunities. However, many of the telecommuting nursing jobs is for in-home care, but there are a few call center jobs for nurses.

**Medco Health Solutions**
(http://www.flexjobs.com/jobs/telecommuting-jobs-at-medco_health_solutions)

Headquartered in New Jersey, Medco Health Solutions, Inc. is a leading pharmacy benefit manager with the nation's largest mail order pharmacy operations. Through advanced pharmacy, Medco improves the health and lowers the total cost of care for clients and their members. If you would like to help improve pharmaceuticals for thousands of consumers around the world and want to join the Medco team as a home based professional, consider one of the telecommuting job leads posted here.

> MAY EVERY SUNRISE HOLD MORE PROMISE, AND EVERY SUNSET HOLD MORE PEACE.
> ·BLESSING·

# PHYSICIANS

**About.com Health Channel**
(http://workathomemoms.about.com/od/medicalandnursingjob1/tp/Work-At-Home-Physician-Jobs.htm)

About.com contracts with more than 600 guides who are experts in their fields to write online content from Home. They are paid a minimum of $675/month to start. However, compensation
increases with page view Growth. Nurses and physicians are often hired as Guides in Health Channel. Additionally, a medical review board that oversees content works remotely.

**Aetna** (http://www.aetna.com/about-aetna-insurance/aetna-careers/)

This major insurance company hires nurses and physicians to work from home. While some positions are specifically designed for telework, in others telework opportunities will be considered. Search jobs database with keyword "telework."

**American Well** (http://www.americanwell.com/careers.html)

Boston-based company, which offers telehealth consultations, online practices, clinical collaboration and medical mobile apps to patients, providers and employers, hires MDs and RNs.

**Covance** (http://jobsearch.covance.com/Physician-jobs.aspx)

This U.S.-based biopharmaceutical development services company, or a contract research organization, has preclinical and clinical research operations in more than 25 countries and more than 10,000 employees worldwide. It hires clinical research associates to work from home and physicians as medical directors in specific locations in the U.S., Canada and Europe. Use "home-based" to search its jobs database.

**Humana** (https://www.humana.com/about/careers/)

Some of the work-at-home positions in this major health care company have geographic requirements. Most are for registered nurses but it sometimes has opportunities for medical coders, chart auditors, licensed insurance reps, accountants, physicians, writers and sales people.

**Imaging On Call**
(http://www.imagingoncall.com/about/teleradiology-jobs/)

BENEFITS OF TELERADIOLOGY CAREERS – FOR DOCTORS
Flexibility in scheduling and lifestyle
Freedom to travel
Competitive compensation and bonuses
Ability to work from the comfort of your own home, wherever you choose to live
Opportunity to learn from a wide variety of interesting cases not normally seen by radiologists at small facilities.

Imaging On Call is always seeking high quality radiologists. If you think a career in teleradiology job is right for you, we want to hear from you. Applicants must be certified by the American Board of Radiology and Fellowship training is preferred. State license(s) are required to practice teleradiology.

IMAGING ON CALL OFFERS EXCITING TELERADIOLOGY CAREERS – FOR DOCTORS
Professional team environment with a close, family atmosphere
Flexible schedules
Bonus system for accurate and productive radiologists
Company paid malpractice insurance

Full time, in-house credentialing staff to assist with medical staff appointments and licensing

**McKesson** (http://www.mckesson.com/careers/careers/)
The nation's largest health care services company, McKesson specializes in pharmaceutical distribution and health care IT systems and software. It hires nurses and physicians in nonclinical work-at-home jobs.

**MedCases**
(http://workathomemoms.about.com/od/medicalandnursingjob1/tp/Work-At-Home-Physician-Jobs.htm)

Providing continuing medical education (CME), this company develops peer-reviewed, case-based, medical education initiatives for physicians, students and other health care practitioners. Remote Medical International The "remote" in the name of Seattle-area company refers to faraway places, not necessarily working at home. However, the company does have a telemedicine department and some other telecommuting jobs.

**Permedion**
(http://hmspermedion.com/careers/physician-reviewers/)

We seek qualified physicians of every specialty to be part of our physician reviewer panel. Requirements to join our panel include appropriate licensure, board certification in specialty, and at least five years of active practice in your specialty in the United States. Contracted as needed, our panel of independent and external medical review physicians performs a variety of reviews, including medical necessity, utilization review, and overall quality evaluation on a variety of cases. All documentation and material for review is sent directly to the physician reviewer.

**Professional Dynamics**
(http://workathomemoms.about.com/od/medicalandnursingjob1/tp/Work-At-Home-Physician-Jobs.htm)

Medical work at home jobs include: Nurses, physicians Case Management California-based Company provides service in the workers compensation industry, and to first- party medical and employee benefit sectors. Some nurse case manager and physician peer review positions are telecommuting.

**Virtual Medical Group** (http://www.virtualmedicalgroup.com/join.html)
Board certified physicians connect with patients via videoconferencing, telephone, and Internet chat, consulting with and possibly writing prescriptions for patients in the states in which they are licensed.

**Vrad** (http://corporate.vrad.com/Careers.aspx)

This company, formerly known as Virtual Radiologic Teleradiology Services, is a provider of teleradiology services and solutions. It hires radiologists to work from home.
Requirements include ABR or ABOR certification; hold at least one state license, eligible for hospital credentialing and available high-speed internet access. Full medical liability insurance is provided.

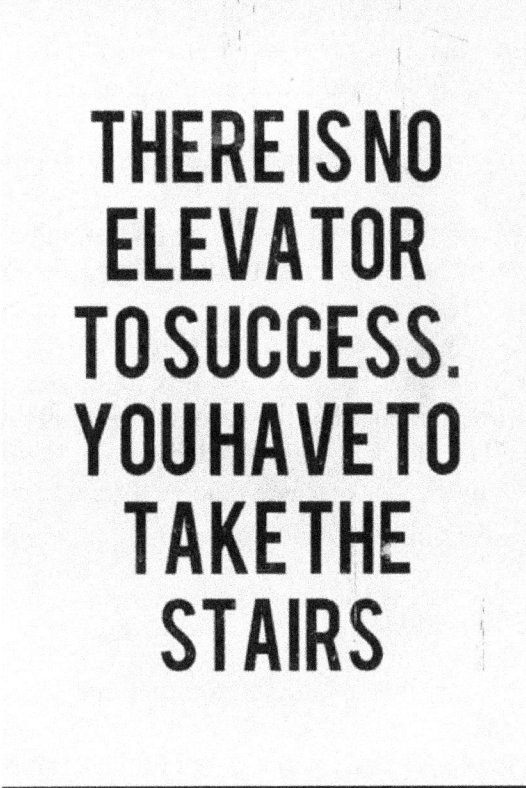

# JURORS

**e-Jury.com** (http://www.ejury.com/)

eJury uses "eJurors" to review cases and deliver their opinions in the form of a verdict. Payment for each verdict is $5-$10, by PayPal. When new cases are up for review, eJury notifies all eligible eJurors, who may then sign into the website to access the details of the proposed lawsuit. Participants are accepted on a first come, first served basis, so it is wise to act quickly once you receive the email notification. The sign up form for ejury.com will take you an estimated five minutes to fill out and you must be comfortable giving out a few personal details such as driver's license number, political party affiliation and city and state of birth.

**JuryTest.Net** (http://www.jurytest.net/index.cfm?action=howjur)

Jurors for JuryTest.net may be asked to provide their opinions on legal cases in several ways, including online questionnaires, recorded voice feedback via a toll-free phone number, online chat room discussions, or teleconferences (also by way of a dial-in 800 number) in which he or she will discuss the case with other jurors for the researchers to witness live. Payments vary according to length of the case, but typically range from $5 to $50 and can be paid by check or PayPal. Please note: In order to participate in the paid mock jury research studies through JuryTest.net, you must have RealPlayer installed and operational on your computer.

**Jury Talk** (www.jurytalk.com)

JuryTalk.com, which is run by the Wilmington Institute Network, a trial and settlement psychology firm, is looking for Research Jurors to provide opinions on current legal cases and participate in focus groups or mock trials. Many of the research studies can be completed online; others require participation at their research facilities in Houston or Dallas, Texas. The sign up form for this paid mock jury site is very quick and easy.

**OnlineVerdict.com** (http://www.onlineverdict.com/jurors.php)

Act as a prospective juror and review cases for payment of $20 to $60 per case. Sign up and when your profile matches a lawyers need you will be invited to sit on the "virtual jury."

**Trial Practice.com** (http://signupdirect.com/)

Sign up to be a mock juror and get paid $100-$150 if you are selected. However, this is not an online review of a case but a live one so you would have to travel outside the home for the 8-10 hour session.

**Trial Juries** (www.trialjuries.com)

The online jury review opportunities for mock jurors offered by TrialJuries.com vary in length as they do with most other mock jury sites, but will usually take about an hour commitment of your time. Rate of pay is typically $30, with the chance to make more for longer or more complex cases. Participants are paid via PayPal.

**Virtual JuryTM (**virtualjury.com)

VirtualJury.com is currently accepting application for mock jurors to participate in online focus groups. The website does not offer much information for jurors upfront; it only states that once you've signed up, you will be notified of any studies you are invited to, and that compensation details will be provided at that time. Payments will be in the form of written checks which will be mailed to jurors within two weeks of their participation.

> ANYONE WHO HAS NEVER MADE A MISTAKE HAS NEVER TRIED ANYTHING NEW

# EDUCATION

**AdmissionsConsultants**
(http://www.admissionsconsultants.com/employment.asp)

Type of Job: admissions
Based in Vienna, VA, AdmissionsConsultants hires candidates with admissions committee experience and good interpersonal skills as consultants for its work at home jobs.

**Aim-for-A Tutoring** (http://www.aim4a.com/tutors.php)

Type of Job: Online Tutoring
Online tutors teach a variety of subjects, including math, science and English, as well as test preparations for GED, PSAT, SAT, GRE, GMAT and AP for students from around the world who range in age from elementary school to college. Teaching experience and a college degree in a subject taught is required.

**American Public University System** (http://www.apus.edu/hiring/)

Type of Job: Online Adjunct Faculty
Encompassing American Public University (APU) and American Military University (AMU), this online Higher education institution hires adjunct faculty members as well as a few administrative positions as Work at home jobs. Master's degree in subject matter is required.
Experience in college-level teaching And/or PhD is preferred.

**Argosy Public University System**
(http://online.argosy.edu/about/employment.aspx)

Type of Job: Online Adjunct Faculty
This college with online education and brick-and-mortar campuses hires online adjunct Faculty to teach graduate and undergraduate courses. Master's or doctoral degree required for these online teaching jobs.

**Auralog**
(http://www.flexjobs.com/jobs/telecommuting-jobs-at-auralog,_inc.)

**Type of Job: Adult** Education, Language
Offers online teaching jobs for language tutors to work in conjunction with its "TeLL me More" language software.

**Brain Mass**
(http://www.flexjobs.com/jobs/telecommuting-jobs-at-brainmass)

Type of Job: Online Teaching Assistants
Register as an online teaching assistant (master's degree or PhD required) in a subject, then answer questions posted by students. The TA earns a percentage of the fee paid by the questioner and can earn more if the answer is downloaded by other students.
Pay in Canadian dollars) is monthly when teaching assistant has earned at least $50 CAD.

**California Virtual Academies**
(http://www.k12.com/cava/a/who-we-are/career-opportunities#.UqNDSyehlicCaliforniaVirtualAcademies)

Type of Job: K-12, Special Education, Language
A network of public charter schools that provides education for students in the state of California. California Virtual Academies hires certified K-12 teachers in California to work from home. In-person meetings in county of employment are required.

**Capella University**
(http://www.capellaeducation.com/capella_careers/capella_careers_index.aspx)

Type of Job: Online Faculty and Instructors
Typical work-at-home at this online college including faculty chairs, core faculty, adjunct faculty, dissertation mentors and channel partner.
Search for positions with an "offsite" location.

**Classof1** (http://classof1.com/careers)

Type of Job: Online Tutoring
Indian company offers online tutoring, homework assistance, test prep, content development and e-learning courses aimed at college and K-12 students in the U.S., U.K. and Australia.
Subjects include math, science, English, social studies, technology, accounting, journalism medicine, engineering, business, economics and more.

**Indeed.com**
Search Indeed.com for "online teaching" for current job postings

**Connections Academy**
(https://www.connectionsacademy.com/careers/home.aspx)

Types of Education-Related Jobs: K-12 Tutoring
Connections Academy, a '"school without walls," is a virtual educational program serving K-12 students throughout various states in a non-classroom-based environment. It hires certified teachers for online teaching jobs.

**Coursebridge**
(http://www.coursebridge.com/html/instructor_application.asp)

Types of Education-Related Jobs: Adult Education, Online Courses
Company offers online courses for adult education. Instructors are paid 55-70 percent of the registration fee per student.

**Creative English Solutions (CES)**
(http://www.englishsolutions.ca/ces_jobs.php)

Types of Education-Related Jobs: Test Writing
Canadian company CES develops practice tests for TOEFL and TOEIC. It hires experienced test writers and voice actors from Canada.

**Educate, Inc.** (Sylvan Learning Centers)
(http://educate-inc.com/careers/top.htm)

Types of Education-Related Jobs: Online Tutoring in K-12, management, sales Parent company of Sylvan Learning Centers, has some corporate telecommuting jobs working as a Liaison between its tutors and clients. Additionally, some of the individual learning centers may offer work-at-home positions for its on-site tutors.

**eduFire** (http://edufire.com/why_teach)

Types of Education-Related Jobs: Adult Education, Languages, Exam Prep
This company doesn't hire online tutors but provides a service of putting together students and tutors and providing online tools for tutoring. It charges a 15 percent commission on all fees collected by tutors.

**EduwizardS** (http://www.eduwizards.com/careers.php)

Types of Education-Related Jobs: Online Tutoring at K-12 and College Level
Company hires freelance tutors and salaried tutors. K-12 tutors in math, science English/reading in the Supplemental Education Services (SES)

and No Child Left Behind (NCLB) program are paid an hourly rate of around $20. U.S. residency and state teaching certification required. Freelance tutors pay a fee to be listed.

**Edu Writers** (http://eduwriters.com/index.html)

Who We Are:
In business since 1998, we have provided thousands of people with the help that they need for school and for their professional lives.

What We Do:
We provide custom research, writing and editing services to students and professionals.

The Benefits of Working For Us:
Working from home, our freelance writers earn from $7 to $15 per page and receive a substantial income. We give our writers the freedom to choose what and when they want to write, allowing writers to set their own schedule based on the deadlines they choose.

What We Are Looking For:
Customer service and repeat clientele are our company's priorities. We are looking for writers who understand the requirements of our priorities by showing us that they can be extremely accurate and always meet deadlines. A college degree is required. All majors are welcomed and encouraged to apply. Our writers research, write and edit papers on a variety of topics from business and agriculture to computer science and biology. Knowledge of various writing styles and documentation is not required, but will be taken into high consideration during the application process. We also hire internationally; however, all applicants must have an impeccable command of English.

What We Are Not Looking For:
Many people start to work for us and for some reason, they think that they can plagiarize their assignments. They cut and paste sections or even whole pages of websites. And we are forced to do the same thing: get rid of them. We have developed software that checks all writing for plagiarism. If we find it, we will notify the writer that he or she does not work for us any longer. We are an employer and we expect our independent contractors to work. So, if you are thinking, "What an easy gig. I can just take stuff off the Net," please do not waste our or your time.

Employment:
If offered a writing position, you will be considered as an independent contractor of the company and will be responsible for reporting any taxes to the Federal Government. You also will be required to sign a contract

with the company regarding company policies. All employees residing within the United States of America are required to complete Internal Revenue Service form W-9, Request for Taxpayer Identification Number and Certification. Information provided within this form is checked for accuracy.

**ETS**
(http://www.ets.org/scoring_opportunitieshttp://www.ets.org/scoring_opportunities)

Types of Education-related jobs: constructed-response scoring professionals who evaluate written short answers or essays, spoken responses and portfolios as part time employees to read for The College Board's Advanced Placement (AP) testing programs and raters for the TOEIC, TOEFL, Praxis and GRE programs. Work schedules vary throughout the year and may take place online and At scoring sites throughout the United States.

**E-Tutor World**
(http://www.etutorworld.net/careers.html)

Types of Education-Related Jobs: Sales, Tutoring
Sales associates for eTutorWorld choose work their work schedules for these work from home jobs, promoting online tutoring services in math and science for school students in grades 5 to 12.
No financial investment required. Free training.

**gofluent** (http://www.gofluent.com/web/us/jobs-in-the-north-america)

Types of Education-Related Jobs: Adult Education, Language
Teaching English by phone, gofluent seeks home-based trainers who are native English speakers who are Bilingual in French, Italian, German, Russian and Korean.
They are hired only from Kansas, Missouri, New York, Oregon, Pennsylvania and Canada.

**Homework Tutoring** (http://www.homeworkhelp.com/tutorjoinus.php)

Types of Education-Related Jobs: Online Tutoring for High School and College
Online tutoring service offers homework help for high school and college students in a variety of subjects.
Emails resume to be considered for these home-based jobs.

**Herzing University** (http://www.herzing.edu/careers-herzing)

Types of Education-Related Jobs: Online Adjunct Faculty
At this online college based in Wisconsin, most of the positions listed as "remote" are for online adjunct Faculty. However, other positions allow telecommuting, but many require time in the office as well.

**Instructional Connections**
(http://www.instructionalconnections.org/employment/)

Types of Education-Related Jobs: Online Coach/Teaching
Assistants, Course Development
Company provides instructional support to colleges. Online coaches, who are part-time, independent contractors, work with students and faculty, monitoring engagement, grading assignments and facilitating course discussions. Pay is based on a per-student, per-course
formula. Master's degree or higher required. Subjects include nursing, education (literacy, reading specialization, special education, bilingual education, educational law, educational administration and mathematics or science education), mathematics, chemistry and biology.

**ITT Technical Institute** (http://www.itt-tech.edu/employment.cfm)

Types of Education-Related Jobs: Online Instructors
Indiana-based technical school offers online as well as on-campus learning in technology, criminal justice, business, and nursing. Online instructors follow an approved curriculum, rather than developing the courses.
Use "online" as the keyword searching all locations.

**Johns Hopkins Center for Talented Youth (CTY)**
(http://cty.jhu.edu/jobs/)

Types of Education-Related Jobs: K-12 Online Tutoring
Instructors critique student writing, make assignments, compose progress reports and evaluations for students in grades 3 to 12. Requirements include BA in appropriate field and at least one year teaching experience. Search CTY or "work at home" in JHU Jobs database.

**Kaplan** (http://www.kaplan.com/careers-at-kaplan/career-areas)

Types of Education-Related Jobs: Online Tutoring, College Instructors, ISDs, Sales Reps Education company Kaplan has work at home openings for college-level online instructors, instructional designers and SAT tutors. Use "virtual" as the keyword in the job search database.

**Laureate Education, Inc.**
(http://www.laureate.net/AboutLaureate/Careers)

Types of Educated-related Jobs: College-Level Course Development, Instructional Design, Management
Laureate Education Inc. is the developer of online education at Walden University, Kendall College, NewSchool of Architecture & Design, College of Santa Fe, and Laureate Higher Education Group.
Most jobs require at least a master's. Choose "Virtual" as job location.

**Manhattan GMAT** (http://www.manhattangmat.com/jobs.cfm)

Types of Education-Related Jobs: Test prep tutoring
Company offers tutors "live courses, online courses and private tutoring students" and pays them $100 an hour for teaching (less during training). The focus of this company which has locations nationwide in the United States as well as in Canada, England and France, is on-site, but there are online jobs as well.

**Nimblemind** (http://nhwaa.com/jobsd-1096-.html)

Types of Education-Related Jobs: Adult Education Course Development and Instruction Design and teach online courses in your area of expertise. Company says "software, instructional technology training and on-going instructor mentoring is provided free of charge" and that it has a "generous "compensation for these independent contractor positions.

**Parliment Tutors** (http://www.parliamenttutors.com/career.php)

Types of Education-Related Jobs: K-12 Online Tutoring Including SAT, GRE Prep and AP subjects New York company hires both in-home and online tutors in the United States.

**Pearson** (http://jobs.pearson.com/go/All-Jobs/329643/)

Types of Education-Related Jobs: High School Level Essay Scoring, Test Development Scorers must have a bachelor's degree or higher, experience teaching high school English, reside and be authorized to work in the U.S. and have access to a private, secure computer with Internet connection. In test development, Pearson hires freelancers to write, do graphic design and review tests.

**Quarasan** (http://www.quarasan.com/careers.html)

Types of Education-Related Jobs: Writing/Editing
Educational publisher hires writers and editors for work at home jobs. Many jobs require teaching experience and/or certification.

**SMARTHINKING.com**
(https://careers-smarthinking.icims.com/jobs/intro?hashed=0)

Types of Education-Related Jobs: Online Tutoring
The Washington, D.C.-based education organization hires part-time (usually 9-20 hours per week), work at home tutors for students of varying abilities and ages. Tutors may work from anywhere in the world as long as they have computer and Internet access (and a U. S. bank account). Peak season for hiring is May-August and November-December every year. Most tutors are paid on an hourly basis. Paid training. Hires graduate and undergraduate students, high school teachers and other experienced tutors.

**Southern New Hampshire University**
(http://www.snhu.edu/online-degrees/adjunct-faculty-ositions.asp)

Types of Education-Related Jobs: Online Adjunct Faculty
Private university in New Hampshire hires online adjunct faculty for undergraduate and graduate courses.
Most courses are already designed and faculty members facilitate learning. However, some courses are instructor-designed. These courses pay $2,200 to $2,500 for 8-and-11-week classes. Online training is provided.

**Teach for America** (http://www.teachforamerica.org/join-our-staff)

Types of Education-Related Jobs: Online Tutoring Management
This non-profit values the virtual workplaces, though obviously its classroom teaching jobs are not work at home. However many of the management jobs can be telecommuted from anywhere in the United States. Management jobs often require teaching experience.

**TutaPoint.com** (http://www.tutapoint.com/info/tutor)

Types of Education-Related Jobs: Online Tutoring
High school level online tutors in Math, science and Spanish must be enrolled in (or have graduated) from an American or Canadian college or university and be available to work from 2 p.m. to 1 a.m., Eastern Standard Time. Pay begins at $12 per hour in addition to incentives. Tutors, who are independent contractors must
commit to at least 5 hours per week. U.S. residents only

**Tutor.com**
(http://www.tutor.com/apply/what-our-tutors-do)
(http://www.homeworkhelp.com/tutorjoinus.php)

Types of Education-Related Jobs: K-12 Online Tutoring
This online teaching service connects students to tutors from computers in their local library, Community center, school, after school program, or from home. To become certified as an online tutor. You must have a degree from or be enrolled in a U.S. or Canadian college, and then you must pass a test in your areas of specialty and submit a writing sample. The process takes 1-3 weeks.

**Sylvan Learning Centers**
(http://tutoring.sylvanlearning.com/sylvan_about_us.cfm)

Types of Education-Related Jobs: Online Tutoring K-12
While many of the opportunities for certified teachers at Sylvan are based in offices, there is some work from home opportunities for tutors once established at a center as well as some corporate home-based positions as well.

**Tutorvista.com** (http://www.tutorvista.com/howitworks.php)

Types of Education-Related Jobs**:** K-12 Tutoring, College-Level Tutoring
Hires experienced teachers with graduate degrees usually from outside the U.S. for part-time and full-time openings.

**UniversalClass** (http://teachonline.universalclass.com/index.htm)

Types of Education-Related Jobs: Adult Education Course Writing, *Online Instructors*
Company provides online continuing education courses to schools, libraries, companies, educators and individuals. It hires instructional writers to author courses on a variety of subjects.
Pays $.04-$.07 per word for writing of course material. Online instructors need a 4-year degree and 4-6 years of work experience in field, and teaching certification and online teaching experience is preferred.

**University of California Berkeley Online Extension**
(http://extension.berkeley.edu/static/about/jobs/teaching/)

Types of Education-Related Jobs: Adult Education, Online Course Instructors, College-Level minimum of master's degree is required but for some courses a doctorate is required.
Experience with Online education is preferred.

**University of Phoenix**
(http://www.phoenix.edu/faculty/become-a-faculty-member.html)

Types of Education-Related Jobs: Online faculty, instructional design
Faculty for this online college needs a master's degree or doctorate in teaching subject as well as working experience in the subject. Jobs are part time (10-20 hours/week). Company also has corporate jobs in instructional design and other education-related fields, but many of these are on-site positions.

**Virtual University**
(http://www.flexjobs.com/jobs/online-college-university)

Types of Education-Related Jobs: Adult Education, Online Courses
Write an online course on subjects as varied as java, meditation, journalism, poetry, personal finance and e-commerce and receive a $200 honorarium.

**Western Governors University**
(http://www.wgu.edu/about_WGU/employment/online_faculty_jobs)

Types of Education-Related Jobs: Distance Learning Mentors
Online college hires mentors to oversee distance-learning students' progress.
Minimum requirement is a bachelor's degree, but master's or doctoral degree and relevant industry experience are preferred.

# TRANSCRIPTION (not medical)

**Aberdeen**
(http://workathomemoms.about.com/od/dataentrytranscription/fl/Work-at-HOme-Company-Profile-Aberdeen-captioning.htm)

Company provides captioning, transcription and translation services and hires transcribers, real time captioners, editors and translators to work at home and in its office in Orange County, CA.
Transcription jobs pay $1-$1.50 per audio minutes; real time captioners are paid $75/hour.

**AccuTran Global**
(http://www.flexjobs.com/jobs/telecommuting-jobs-at-accutran_global)

Transcribe conference calls, meetings and interviews for the financial sector in this Canadian company's home transcription jobs. It hires transcribers as independent contractor on a part-time basis.
Pay ranges from $0.005 to $0.0066 per word. 70 WPM preferred for most jobs. Other jobs available include transcription reviewer, editor, real-time writer or captioner, formatter and supervisor. Hires in U.S., U.K. and Canada.

**Alice Darling Audio Transcription Services**
(http://www.alicedarling.com/about/employment.html)

Boston-area company hires experienced transcriptionists to work from home or from its offices. Company's clients are in the fields of science, biotechnology, academia, business, technology, finance, Medicine, film, advertising and the law.
70 WPM required for transcription jobs.

American High-Tech Transcription and Reporting
(http://www.htsteno.com/jobs.html)
Firm offering transcription and translation services to government, law enforcement, corporations and other organizations hires both on-site and work-at-home transcriptionists.
Applicants must pass and pay for FBI and state criminal background checks with fingerprints.

**Capital Typing** (http://www.capitaltyping.com/employment-application)

Outsourcing company based in South Carolina provides virtual office services.
In addition to its data entry and transcription jobs from home, it offers online customer support, translation and secretarial services.

**Clark Fork Communications**
(http://workathomemoms.about.com/od/dataentrytranscription/p/Clark-Fork-)

This company mostly hires experienced legal and corporate transcriptionists (though it does sometimes have basic data entry jobs). Legal transcription rate is $0.75 to $1.75 per page, and corporate ranges from $0.40 to $1.00 per audio minute.
Must be a U.S. citizen. Background check may be required.

**Cyber Dictate** (http://www.cyberdictate.com/company/employment/)
Recruits U.S. citizens as independent contractors for transcription jobs.
Minimum of 70 WPM and 2 years of experience required.
Hires both legal and general transcriptionists.

**DionData Solutions** (http://www.diondatasolutions.net/opportunities.htm)
Hires typists with a minimum of 60 wpm and basic computer skills for home transcription jobs. No fees.

**e-Typist.com**
(http://www.e-typist.com/Employment_work_at_home-dictation-service.htm)
Company hires work at home transcriptionists for legal and insurance-rated transcription jobs. Submit resume and company will contact applicants when it has openings. 60 WPM and knowledge of legal terms required.

**Morningside Partners**
(http://www.flexjobs.com/jobs/telecommuting-jobs-at-orningide_partners_llc)

Morningside produces verbatim transcripts of broadcast programming that Appears on CNN, FOX News, MSNBC and CNBC. It hires at-home Transcribers.
Requirements for home transcription jobs include high-speed Internet connection; digital foot pedal system; bachelor's degree in English or journalism and at least three years of work experience.

**Mountain West Processing**
(http://www.flexjobs.com/jobs/telecommuting-jobs-at-mountain_west_Processing)
Company hires independent contractors to work as legal, corporate, general and Medical transcriptionists. Rates for these transcription jobs may be per page, per audio minute or per word.

**Mulberry Studio** (http://www.mulberrystudio.com/mainsite/jobs.html)

Company offers full- and part-time transcription and proofreading positions either on-site in Cambridge, MA, or on a freelance basis from home. Typing speed of 75 wpm, excellent grammar and language skills, and two years of experience in transcription and word processing are required.

**Neal R. Cross & Company**
(http://www.nealrgross.com/transcriber-employment-details)

Neal R. Gross & Co. is a Washington, DC based court reporting and transcription company. We have been in business over 35 years and provide verbatim court reporting and transcription services to a broad range of government and private clients.

REQUIREMENTS:

MUST TYPE AT LEAST 60 WPM
EXCELLENT COMMAND OF ENGLISH LANGUAGE
MUST BE ABLE TO WORK A MINIMUM OF 30 HOURS PER WEEK
If you type over 60 words per minute and need to work from home, you may be what we're looking for in a legal transcriber. No transcription experience necessary, but you must be willing and able to work on overnight delivery. Timeliness is a must, as are excellent English language skills. Please apply only if you can transcribe at least 5 hours of audio per week.

Most of our recordings are digital, so please indicate in your resume or cover letter if you are familiar with digital audio and with using an FTP program.

To inquire about taking a transcription test for this position, please send a cover letter and resume to: transcribe@nealrgross.com.

All NRGCO transcribers are independent (1099) Subcontractors.

**Net Transcripts**
(http://www.nettranscripts.com/careers.htm)
*Law Enforcement Transcriber*

Individuals who can transcribe audio content of criminal investigations, internal affairs, and patrol reports. You must have prior experience transcribing for a law enforcement agency (police department, sheriff's department, etc.), type 80+ WPM, have excellent grammar, outstanding accuracy and proofreading skills, have experience with MS Word, and must demonstrate strong computer literacy.

A full criminal background check is required for individuals completing this work.

There is an initial assessment period before any individual is able to complete client work. Therefore, it is essential that you have prior Law Enforcement transcription experience and be able to proof your work to be at least 99% accurate.

*General Transcriber*

Individuals who can transcribe audio content of financial results conferences, medical training seminars, group project meetings and other general business meetings. Must type 80+ WPM, have excellent grammar and proofreading skills, have experience with MS Word and Excel, and must demonstrate strong computer literacy.

There is an initial assessment period before any individual is able to complete client work. Therefore, you should have prior experience in transcription. Those most successful candidates will have had work experience creating, reviewing or interpreting corporate financial information (e.g. 10Q, 10K, Annual Reports).

**QuickTate or iDictate** (http://typists.quicktate.com/transcribers/signup)

Company provides transcription of short audio files such as voicemails and dictated notes by hiring Work-at-home transcribers. Quicktate pays $.0025 per word (this pay may vary—see their website).
Successful Quicktate transcriptionists may receive work from iDictate which transcribes a wider range of documents. Bilingual, particularly Spanish-language transcribers are needed.

**Scribie** (https://scribie.com/freelance-transcription#intro)
Freelance transcriptionists choose audio files to transcribe at $10 per audio hour.
Files are 6 minutes or less. Opportunity for advancement to reviewer.

**SpeakWrite**
(http://www.speakwrite.com/WEB/sw/employment/typist/typist-home.aspx)
Hiring home-based typists throughout the United States and Canada to work as independent contractors.
SpeakWrite requires a typing speed of 65 WPM for its transcription jobs.

**Talk2Type Transcriptions** (http://www.talk2type.net/transcriber.html)
Independent contractors must type at least 75 wpm and have their own Equipment to qualify for this telecommuting position

**Terescription**
(http://www.terescription.com/site/terescriber/terescriberSignUp.aspx)

Independent contractors transcribe for the entertainment industry. A foot Pedal is required. Work pays $.07/line for a one-person interview and potentially more for multiple-speaker interviews.
A transcriber typing at 70wpm can earn between $12 and $15 per hour.

Terescription provides affordable and professional transcription services for the entertainment, business, legal and educational markets.

(At the time of this printing, this company said they have all the transcribers they need but did say they would accept applications and contact you when there is an opening).

**Fantastic Transcripts**
(http://www.fantastictranscripts.com/employment.html)

Fantastic Transcripts is a fantastic place to work. We offer a casual work environment in our downtown Boston offices.

We also offer great flexibility in scheduling - work when you want to - and the Pepsi is free.

With Suffolk University and Emerson College only a block away, our part-time jobs are perfect for mature students with typing and transcription skills.

Our central location at the intersection of five transit lines also makes us easy to get to from just about anywhere in the metropolitan area.

You must type a minimum of 60 words per minute, transcribe a minimum of 35 words per minute, be comfortable using a computer, and you must pass a transcription aptitude test taken in our offices. We pay $10 to $12 to start, and overtime after 40 hours if we really get busy.

Our office is standardized on Windows XP and Microsoft Word 2000 with documents saved in the Word 95 format standard.

To apply, please e-mail your resume to us at jobs@fantastictranscripts.com and include your typing speed. If your background meets with what we are looking for, we will contact you to set up a time for an interview and a transcription test.

Freelance Transcriptionists
We are always interested in hearing from experienced transcriptionists to work on a sub-contract, freelance basis from your home or office.

When contacting us, please let us know what you charge to transcribe an hour's worth of audio because this is how we charge our clients.

To figure out your per hour of audio charge, estimate how long it usually takes you to transcribe an hour of audio and then multiply that number by what an hour of your time is worth.

E-mail your resume and background information to us at jobs@fantastictranscripts.com and we will consider you for future work.

Fantastic Transcripts is a fantastic place to work. We offer a casual work environment in our downtown Boston offices.

We also offer great flexibility in scheduling - work when you want to - and the Pepsi is free.

With Suffolk University and Emerson College only a block away, our part-time jobs are perfect for mature students with typing and transcription skills.

Our central location at the intersection of five transit lines also makes us easy to get to from just about anywhere in the metropolitan area.

You must type a minimum of 60 words per minute, transcribe a minimum of 35 words per minute, be comfortable using a computer, and you must pass a transcription aptitude test taken in our offices. We pay $10 to $12 to start, and overtime after 40 hours if we really get busy.

Our office is standardized on Windows XP and Microsoft Word 2000 with documents saved in the Word 95 format standard.

To apply, please e-mail your resume to us at jobs@fantastictranscripts.com and include your typing speed. If your background meets with what we are looking for, we will contact you to set up a time for an interview and a transcription test.

Freelance Transcriptionists
We are always interested in hearing from experienced transcriptionists to work on a sub-contract, freelance basis from your home or office.

When contacting us, please let us know what you charge to transcribe an hour's worth of audio because this is how we charge our clients.

To figure out your per hour of audio charge, estimate how long it usually takes you to transcribe an hour of audio and then multiply that number by what an hour of your time is worth.

E-mail your resume and background information to us at jobs@fantastictranscripts.com and we will consider you for future work.

# LANGUAGE TRANSLATION

## Bi-lingual call center

### 1-800-FLOWERS
(http://ww30.1800flowers.com/template.do?id=template8&page=9000&conversionTag=true)

New York-based floral company regularly hires for at-home call center jobs on a temporary basis for seasonal employment. It does occasionally hire permanent (particularly bilingual), at-home call center agents as well. Must live in the following states: Florida, New Mexico, New York, Ohio, Oklahoma, Texas or Virginia.

**Advanis** (http://www.advanis.ca/available-positions)

Canadian market research company hires for virtual call center jobs and mystery shopping jobs.
Bilingual jobs in French or Spanish available for the home call center jobs. Must live in Canada for call center jobs

**Alpine Access** (https://jobs.alpineaccess.com/)

Home-based agents take in-bound customer service and sales call for various clients.
Reps at this Business process outsourcer (BPO) are paid at an hourly rate of around $9, and training is paid.
 Requires a minimum commitment of 20 hours per week with up to full-time hours available.
Bilingual jobs in Languages such as Spanish, Mandarin and Cantonese available.

**Apple At-Home Advisors** (http://www.apple.com/jobs/us/aha.html)

Apple at Home is a work at home call center program from Apple that is part of the company's Apple Care department. Use the keyword "home" in the company's job database. It recruits French and English bilingual agents who live within 100 miles of Markham, Ontario.

**American Express**
 (http://jobs.americanexpress.com/key/work-from-home-jobs.html)

The travel division of American Express hires bilingual virtual travel agents and call center agents with experience in reservation systems in the U.S., U.K., Canada and Australia. Use "virtual" "telecommute" or "work at home" as keywords to find a job online in its database.


**Affiliated Computer Services, Inc.** (http://www.acs-inc.com/)

FORTUNE 500 companies, owned by Xerox, provides business process  outsourcing (BPO) and Information technology solutions. Company offers part-time employment (paying $10/hr) for home call center agents, bilingual (Spanish) preferred.
Use "work at home" a keyword in company's careers database.

**BSG - Third Party Verification**
(http://www.bsgclearing.com/contact_us/careers/)

Agents take inbound calls to do third party verification for utility, cable and financial services clients. Agents can choose shifts as short as two hours.  Pay is $8.50/hour for English-only agents and $9/hour for bilingual agents. Languages needed include Korean, Vietnamese, Spanish, Cantonese, Mandarin, Tagalog, Arabic, Armenian, Bosnian, Cantonese, Farsi, German, Indonesian, Korean, Mandarin, Persian, Polish, Somalia, Russian, Turkish, Ukrainian and Yugoslavian.

**Century Link** (http://www.centurylink.com/Pages/AboutUs/CompanyInformation/Careers/)

Formerly CenturyTel and EMBARQ, CenturyLink is a provider of voice, broadband and video services for consumers and businesses in 33 states.
Work at home call center jobs pay around $10-11/per hour.
Bilingual encouraged to apply. Search job database using "work at home."
Work at home jobs are based in FL, IN, KS, MN, MO, NC, NE, NJ, NV, OH, PA, SC, TN, TX, VA, and WY.

**Hilton Hotels** (http://jobs.hiltonworldwide.com/en/?cntry=united-states)

Hotel chain's Hilton@Home program hires motivated, work-from-home sales agents for customer care and reservations. New hires receive in-depth training and support.
Bilingual jobs in Spanish or Portuguese earn $1 per hour more.
$47/hr in Part-time job openings. Requirements: Must have a computer.

**JetBlue** (http://www.jetblue.com/work-here/job-descriptions.aspx)

Airline hires some home-based customer service representatives as employees.
Bilingual ability may be required for some call center jobs. Travel to Salt Lake City, UT, office may be required.

**LiveOps** (http://join.liveops.com/)

Company hires independent-contractor, call-center agents, including licensed Insurance agents, for a variety of positions including outbound sales, bilingual customer service (Spanish and French) and financial services.

**NEW Corp** (https://www.newcorp.com/careers)

Extended warranty company pays home-based customer care reps $9-10 per hour to take in-bound calls. It hires both work-at-home and office-based call center agents to troubleshoot and provide customer service for its clients.
New hires who live within 50 miles of a brick-and-mortar training site must train there; others can train virtually. The company's clients include Best Buy, Lowe's DirecTV, Wal-Mart, GameStop, AT&T and Gateway. Hires agents bilingual in Spanish/English also.

**TeleTech@Home**  (http://www.teletechjobs.com/athome-en-US)

Global business process outsourcing (BPO) company hires associates in some U.S. states and the U.K.  To work from home as call agents and other fields. TeleTech@Home's call center agents are employees, not independent contractors.
These call center agents perform sales, customer service, and technical support.
Agents bilingual in Spanish, German, French, Catalan, Dutch and many other languages are hired.  Pay is $9-10/hour.

**U-Haul**
(http://jobs.uhaul.com/contact_center.aspx?jobtype=workfromhome)

Work at home call center agents take incoming calls from customers dialing specific U-Haul moving centers across the US and Canada. English/French bilingual agents needed in Canada. Representatives answer general questions, take reservation and/or provide roadside assistance. Paid training.

**Ubiqus**
(http://www.ubiqus.com/GB/recruitment.htm)

Ubiqus is an Equal Opportunity Employer. It considers all positions without regard to race, religion, color, sex, national origin, age, disability or other categories as proscribed by federal, state or local law.

Fill out our online application. If we are interested in your credentials, we will contact you by email or telephone:

Note: Transcriptionist Applicants, please read our disclaimer before beginning your application

- Verbatim Transcriptionist
- Medical Transcriptionist
- Summary Writer
- Medical Summary Writer
- Translator
- Interpreter
- Foreign Language Transcriptionist

Audio Technician

Audience Response Technician

**VIP Desk**
(https://www.vipdesk.com/employment/login.aspx?ReturnUrl=%2femployment%2fapplicant%2fmyhomepage.aspx&cc=635220487313204132)

Home shoring company specializes in delivering concierge and virtual call center services for the "high-value customers" of its corporate clients. Its home-based agents handle customer requests via phone, e-mail, and chat and research and fulfill requests from customers in the United States and abroad. Offers full- and part-time hours but agents must commit to certain availabilities.
Fluency in English is required. Fluency in French, German, Spanish or Italian is a plus.

**West at Home** (http://www.apply.westathome.com/applynow.html)

West at Home's customer service agents are employees who handle billing, sales or technical troubleshooting calls for the company's clients. They are paid on a per-minute rate, per-call or minimum wage. Training is paid. Some bilingual jobs are available

**Working Solutions**
 (http://www.workingsolutions.com/work-at-home-agents/)

Company contracts with agents to do call center and data entry jobs for clients.
Pay ranges from $7.20 to $30 an hour. Call center projects include order processing, reservations, Customer service, sales, market research and technical support.
Applicants who successfully complete a two-part online test are placed on a list and notified when a project becomes available. Hires agents Bilingual in 32 different languages including Mandarin, Portuguese, Bengali, Spanish, Italian, French, German, Greek, Vietnamese, Tagalog, Punjabi, Japanese, Hindi, Romanian, Polish, Russia and Arabic.
Accepts agents from outside the U.S. for some projects.

## BI-Lingual work from home jobs:

**1-800-FLOWERS**
(http://ww30.1800flowers.com/template.do?id=template8&page=9000&conversionTag=true)

Bilingual jobs: Call Center
New York-based floral company regularly hires for at-home call center jobs on a temporary basis for seasonal employment. It does occasionally hire permanent (particularly bilingual), at-home call center agents as well. Must live in the following states: Florida, New Mexico, New York, Ohio, Oklahoma, Texas or Virginia.

**Aberdeen**
(http://workathomemoms.about.com/od/dataentrytranscription/fl/Work-at-HOme-Company-Profile-Aberdeen-Captioning.htm)

Bilingual Jobs: Translation, Transcription
Company provides captioning, transcription and translation services and hires transcribers, real time captioners, editors and translators to work at home and in its office in Orange County, CA.
Transcription jobs pay $1-$1.50 per audio minutes; real time captioners are paid $75/hour.

**Acclaro** (http://www.acclaro.com/localization-jobs)

Bilingual Jobs: Localization, translation
Agency hires experienced freelance translators and other localization professionals to work from home.

**Appen Butler Hill**
(http://workathomemoms.about.com/od/translatorsandinterpretor/p/Appen
ButlerHill.htm)

Bilingual Jobs: Translation Review
Hires language consultants and data annotators who evaluate online search results as well as translators and transcriptionists. Looks for candidates with experience in linguistics, especially computational; software testing and library science plus a native-level fluency in more than one language other than English.

**Apple At-Home Advisors** (http://www.apple.com/jobs/us/aha.html)

Bilingual Jobs: Call Center, Tech Support
Apple at Home is a work at home call center program from Apple that is part of the company's Apple Care department. Use the keyword "home" in the company's database. Apple recruits French and English bilingual agents who live within 100 miles of Markham, Ontario.

**1-800-Translate** (http://www.1-800-translate.com/company/jobs/)

Bilingual Jobs: Translation, Interpretation
Hires freelance translators and on-site interpreters. College degree required.
Email resume for consideration. Languages include English, Dutch, Haitian, Creole, Korean, Hebrew, Farsi, Russian, Spanish, Polish, Japanese, Arabic, Mandarin, French, Amharic, Portuguese and more.

**About en Español**
(http://weblogs.about.com/b/2011/09/20/writing-jobs-for-spanish-
bloggers-open-At-about-com.htm)

Bilingual Jobs: Writing
About.com contracts guides, which are experts in many fields, to write online content for its Spanish-language site About en Español. Must be fluent in English and Spanish. Pay for this work at home jobs starts at $675/month.

**AuraLog**
(http://www.flexjobs.com/jobs/telecommuting-jobs-at-auralog,_inc.)

Compensation increases with page view growth.
Bilingual Jobs: Teaching
Hires online language tutors to work in conjunction with "Tell me more" Language software.

**Connections Academy**
(https://www.connectionsacademy.com/careers/home.aspx)

Bilingual Jobs: Teaching
Connections Academy "a school without walls", is a virtual educational program serving K-12 Students throughout various states in a non-Classroom-based environment. It hires certified Teachers for online teaching jobs.
This includes foreign language teacher for K-12 German, French and Spanish.

**CSC** (http://www.csc.com/careersus/flxwd/16005-careers)

Bilingual Jobs: Translation, Media Monitoring
Company offers IT-enabled business solutions and services to businesses. Jobs in its database indicate whether it is remote. Hires for telecommute jobs in IT, management and translation.

**eduFire** (http://edufire.com/why_teach)

Bilingual Jobs: Teaching
Types of Online Teaching Jobs: Adult Education, Languages, Exam Prep (this company does not hire Online tutors but provides a service of putting together students and tutors and providing online tools for tutoring. It charges 15 percent commission on all fees collected by tutors.

**GlobaLink Translations Ltd.**
(http://www.globalinktranslations.com/work_with_us.asp?section=workwithus)

Bilingual Jobs: Translation, Translation Review, Localization
Canadian company assists clients with translation and cultural adaptation needs.
Its translation jobs are for both translators and translation reviewers.

**gofluent** (http://www.gofluent.com/web/us/careers)

Bilingual Jobs: Teaching
Teaching English by phone, gofluent seeks home-based trainer who are native English speaker and are Bilingual in French, Italian, German, Russian and Korean.
They hire only from Kansas, Missouri, New York, Oregon, and Pennsylvania and Canada.

**Google**
(http://workathomemoms.about.com/od/webdesignmarketing/p/Google-Ads-Quality-Rater.htm)

Bilingual Jobs: Translation Review/Quality Rater
Hires ads quality raters who evaluate the accuracy of Google web advertising and communicating the effectiveness of web layouts and information using an online tool.
The requirements include a BA/BS Degree (or equivalent experience); fluency in a specific language as well as English; an understanding of the culture of the speakers of the specific language; web research and analytic capabilities, high-speed Internet connection and U.S. work authorization. Languages include Chinese, Japanese, Korean, Russian, Italian, German, Spanish, Turkish and more.

**LiveOPs** (http://join.liveops.com/being-an-agent/)

Bilingual Jobs: call Center
Company hires independent-contractor, call-center agents, including licensed insurance agents, for a variety of positions including outbound sales, bilingual customer service (Spanish and French) and financial services.

**Language Line Solutions**
(https://www.languageline.com/company/careers/)

Bilingual Jobs: Interpreter
Interpreters are tasked with quickly understanding and instantly communicating an idea across two languages, while retaining the meaning of the original message. This requires a high level of proficiency in both languages because some concepts do not always translate literally from one language to another. A qualified interpreter will be capable of performing this action without delay and in a manner that effectively facilitates the conversation until its completion.

**LanguagesUnlimited** (http://www.languagesunlimited.com/)

Bilingual Jobs: Translation, Interpretation
Company hires linguists on a freelance basis for translation jobs as well as on-site and telephone interpretation and transcription services. To apply, register in company's database.
Languages include Japanese, Chinese, Spanish, English, French, German, Russian, Bengali, Hindi, Portuguese and more.

**Linguistic Systems**
(http://www.linguist.com/for-translators-overview.htm)

Bilingual Jobs: Translation, Interpretation
Requirements include two years experience, college degree, access to email and knowledge of use basic translation software tools. Company seeks "language professionals with in depth knowledge in a professional field (such as medicine, software, finance, and engineering, interpreters or narrators (voice-over professionals) living in the New England area." Online application includes translating a short text for each language pair you wish to qualify in. Permit to work in U.S. required.

**Network Omni** (http://www.networkomni.com/about-careers.asp)

Hires experienced freelance language specialists as independent contractors. Minimum requirements are 3 years professional experience in translation or interpretation, college degree and knowledge in specific subject areas, such as legal and financial matters, marketing writing, medical and general business.
Also have freelance opportunities for desktop publishers and localization engineers.

**Pacific Interpreters** (http://www.pacificinterpreters.com/careers/)

Bilingual Jobs: Translation, Interpretation
Company hires telephonic interpreters and translators for the medical industry. U.S. citizenship/work permit and experience in medical industry required.

**Quicktate/iDictate**
(http://workathomemoms.about.com/od/workathomejobprofiles/p/Quicktate-Idictate.htm)

Bilingual Jobs: Transcription
Company provides transcription of short audio files, such as voicemails and dictated notes, by hiring work-at-home transcribers. Quicktate pays $.0025 per word and iDictate and Quicktates medical transcription work pay $.0050 per word. Successful QuickTate transcriptionists may receive work from iDictate, which transcribes a wider range of documents. Bilingual, particularly Spanish and English, transcribers needed but other languages such as French, Italian, German, Chinese, Farsi, Portuguese and Japanese desired as well.

**SDL** (http://www.sdl.com/aboutus/careers/careers.html)

Bilingual Jobs: Translation
Global information management company hires freelance translators for translation jobs. The company is a supplier of localization services to the IT, engineering, e-business & multimedia sectors, and experience in those and other business sectors are helpful.
Requirements are a minimum 2 years freelance (or 1 year in-house) translation experience, but the company says it accepts "translators with relevant experience.

**SMARTTHINKING.com**
(https://careers-smarthinking.icims.com/jobs/intro)

Bilingual Jobs: Teaching
The Washington, D.C.-based education organization hires part-time (usually 9-20 hours per week), work-at-home tutors for many subjects (including foreign languages) for students of varying abilities and ages. Tutors may work from anywhere in the world as long as they have computer and Internet access (and a U. S. bank account).
Peak season for hiring is May-August and November-December every year. Most tutors are paid on an hourly basis. Paid training.
Hires graduate and undergraduate as well as high school students.

**Telelanguage** (http://www.telelanguage.com/careers)
Bilingual Jobs: Interpretation, Translation
Company offers opportunities for both on-site and telephone interpreters.

**Translators.com** (http://www.translatorscafe.com/cafe/default.asp)
Bilingual Jobs: Interpretation, Translation
Bid site for translation and interpretation services offers thousands of opportunities in a huge variety of Languages.

**VIP Desk**
(http://workathomemoms.about.com/od/companieshiringwahms/p/VIPdesk-Jobs.htm)

Bilingual Jobs: Call Center
Home shoring company specializes in delivering concierge and virtual call center services for the "high-value customers" of its corporate clients. Its home-based agents handle customer requests via phone, e-mail, and chat and research and fulfill requests from customers in the United States and abroad. Offers full- and part-time hours but agents must commit to certain availabilities.
 Fluency in English is required. Fluency in French, German, Spanish or Italian is a plus.

**WordExpress** (http://www.wordexpress.net/freelance-position.html)

Bilingual Jobs: Translation, Interpretation, Desktop Publishing, Sales, Voice Talent Santa Monica, CA-based company hires for freelance translation jobs in more than 100 different languages from anywhere in the world. Other positions include sales managers and reps, interpreters, desktop publishers and voice talent.

**Working Solutions**
(http://www.workingsolutions.com/work-at-home-agents/)

Bilingual Jobs: Call Center
Company contracts with agents to do call center and data entry jobs for clients. Pay ranges from $7.20 to $30 an hour. Call center projects include order processing, reservations, enrollments, customer service, sales, market research and technical support. Applicants who successfully complete a two-part online test are placed on a list and notified when a project becomes available.
Hires agents bilingual in 32 different languages including Mandarin, Portuguese, Bengali, Spanish, Italian, French, German, Greek, Vietnamese, Tagalog, Punjabi, Japanese, Hindi, Romanian, Polish, Russian and Arabic. Accepts agents from outside the U.S., for some projects.

**Indeed.com** (Indeed.com)
Search Indeed.com for bilingual jobs. Read job descriptions carefully because this is an automated search that pulls listings from many sources, and it may pull non-work-from-home jobs too.

**Worldlingo** (http://www.worldlingo.com/en/company/jobs.html)

Bilingual Jobs: Translation, Interpretation, Proofreading, Editing, Writing, Desktop Publishing, Sales, Voice Talent
Requirements for generalist translators or proofreader are 5 years continuous translation experience in a commercial environment, membership of the professional translation association, university degree from a recognized institution and Trados 5 Freelance.

**DialogOne**
(http://dialog-one.com/career/)

Dialog One is committed to delivering the very best cross cultural communication solutions to meet our client's needs. We are always looking for highly skilled professionals and reliable agents such as freelance translators, interpreters, cultural mediators, marketing professionals, desktop publishers, webmaster with foreign language skills and other professionals to help us meet our clients' globalization strategies.

Minimal Qualifications:
Minimum 2 years of College Education
Excellent verbal and written communication
Fluent in both native and acquired languages
Experience working with inter-cultural environments
The ability to pass "Proficiency Exam"
Criminal background check
Drug test
Provide Two (2) letters of recommendations

Dialog One offer numerous advantages:
Opportunities to support in a variety of services and time frames
An agent relations department dedicated to assist while you are collaborating with Dialog One access to work opportunities in a variety of specialties and fields of interest accumulate and balance your work experience with a company that accredits your experience.

# SEARCH EVALUATION

**Appen Butler Hill**
(*www.flexjobs.com/jobs/telecommuting-jobs-at-butler_hill_group)*

Termed "search engine evaluators" at this company, these freelance positions require workers to give feedback to ensure that Internet search results are "accurate, timely, comprehensive, free of spam and relevant to the search query's intent." The evaluators must be native speakers of the language in which they are working and be knowledgeable about the Internet and familiar with a wide variety of online news sources. Contractors in these temporary positions work four hours per day (Monday-Friday).
Jobs require residency in a specific country.

**Butler Hill**
(https://tbe.taleo.net/CH05/ats/careers/requisition.jsp?org=BUTLERHILL&cws=4&rid=213)

*Web search evaluator*
As a Web Search Evaluator at Appen, you will be rewarded for your ability to improve the Internet search relevance results for everyone. Be part of a rapidly growing global team for the world's top Internet search engine companies! We offer flexible work schedules, competitive pay and excellent training.

If you are a fast-thinking, flexible person who embraces new challenges and would enjoy evaluating the quality and relevance of the Internet for our top clients, we want to hear from you. We will provide you with standards and scoring guidelines, personal support and training so you can be successful.

Depending upon your commitment and skill level, opportunities for new projects and responsibilities that can increase your ability to earn are always there for you. We are moving fast … and so can your career. It's all up to you.

**Google** (Workforce Logic)
(http://workathomemoms.about.com/od/webdesignmarketing/p/Google-Ads-Quality-Rater.htm)

Google calls this same position an ads quality rater. It is one of the only work-at-home positions the Internet giant offers, and it doesn't even hire for it directly. It advertises for the positions on its employment page but the hiring is done through WorkForce Logic.
These positions require U.S. residency.

**Lionbridge**
(http://workathomemoms.about.com/od/translatorsandinterpretor/p/Lionbridge.htm)

Global Localization Company has what it terms Internet assessor as well as several other similar jobs in its "crowd sourcing" division. These jobs include:
*Internet assessors who evaluate results of a web search
*Social media search consultants who express opinions on the quality of content
*Internet judges, which are similar to Internet assessor
*In-country financial consultants who monitor and document changes in regulatory requirements and national standards in a given country/market
Online maps specialist who evaluate and improve online mapping software.

**Leapforce**
(https://www.leapforceathome.com/qrp/public/requirements;jsessionid=269388D3780A311AD661B2EA9E1FB27A)

As a Leapforce At Home independent agent, you will enjoy the freedom and flexibility to choose when and the amount of time you work, allowing you to balance your career, family and friends.
Leapforce At Home provides an exciting home-based career opportunity where you can put your acute analytical skills to work, providing valuable feedback and critical insight for some of today's leading companies.
With no set schedules of any kind, Leapforce At Home independent agents enjoy the flexibility to choose how much and when to work.
Successful Leapforce At Home independent agents are smart, inquisitive and dig online research.

Leapforce has made a core promise to our customers to work with only the very best home-based independent agents. Each Leapforce At Home independent agent is an integral part of our shared success and we are very serious about keeping our promise. Leapforce At Home agents conduct in depth internet-based research and provide information evaluation for leading companies from around the globe.
Check out the basic equipment and skills required to become a Leapforce At Home Agent:

Equipment Requirements
High speed internet access (Cable Modem, DSL, etc.)
A personal computer running Mozilla's free Firefox web browser, version 20.x - 26.x.
Up to date anti-virus and anti-spyware software

Basic Skill Requirements
Excellent web research skills and analytical abilities
Excellent comprehension and written communication skills

Many Leapforce agents must pass an assessment test before being hired.

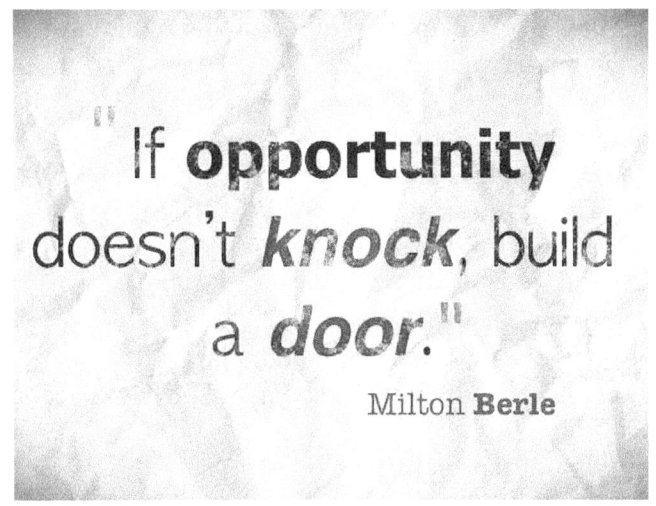

## MICRO TASKS
(THESE TASKS TAKE A SMALL AMOUNT OF TIME TO DO AND PAYS INSTANTLY)


**Amazon Mechanical Turk** (https://www.mturk.com/mturk/welcome)
Type of micro job: Online tasks, crowd sourcing
Pays in: US dollars, Indian rupees or Amazon gift certificates, depending on your location.

**App Rewards** (http://www.apprewardsclub.com/)
Type of micro job: Rewards program for using cell phone apps
Pays in: Points on RewardsDen and Kiip

**Clickworker** (http://www.clickworker.com/en/)
Type of micro job: Crowd sourcing in writing, translating, data entry and research.
Pays in: US dollars or euros, monthly

**ClixSense** (http://www.clixsense.com/en/Tasks)
Type of micro job: Online task site
Pays in: US dollars, twice weekly via PayPal, Payza, Liberty Reserve; month for checks; minimum cash-out requirements with fees.

**CloudCrowd** (http://www.cloudcrowd.com/)
Type of micro job: Crowd sourcing in general writing, marketing writing, and editing (Chicago Manual of Style)
Pays in: US dollars in PayPal account

**CrowdFlower** (https://tasks.crowdflower.com/auth_central/login/new)
Type of micro job: Various
Pays in: USD via PayPay; withdraws require an $84 minimum and can be processed 15 days after payment is made.

**CoinWorker** (http://coinworker.com/)
Type of micro job: Online task site
Pays in Bitcoins (BTC); earn points at 1 point=$0.1USD; at 180, points are converted to bitcoins at the prevailing BTC/USD exchange rate.

**Gigs Bull** (http://gigsbull.com)
Type of micro job: Online task/services marketplace
Pays in: Amounts calculated in USD into a PayPal or Payza account

**EasyShift** (http://easyshiftapp.com/)
Type of micro job: Real-world task site via mobile phone
Pays in: US dollars in PayPal account

**Embee Mobile** (http://embeemobile.com/)
Type of micro job: Mobile micro task websites
Pays in: Points redeemable for mobile airtime or other services

**Fittytown** (http://www.fittytown.com/)
Type of micro job: Online task/services marketplace

**Fiverr** (http://fiverr.com/)
Type of micro job: Online task marketplace
Pay is: Calculated in USD and paid via PayPay with a 2% or $1 fee (whichever is less) in the currencies that PayPal works with.

**Fivesquids** (http://www.fivesquids.co.uk/)
Type of micro job: Online task/services marketplace
Pays in: Pounds via PayPal with a 2% or £1 fee (whichever is less)

**Field Agent** (http://www.fieldagent.net/)
Type of micro job: Real-world and online tasks via mobile phone
Pays in: PayPal account; jobs pay $3-12 each

**Gigwalk** (http://gigwalk.com/)
Type of micro job: Real-world and online micro tasks via mobile phone
Pays in: PayPal account; tasks typically pay $3-5 per gig

**Inbox Dollars** (http://www.inboxdollars.com/members)
Type of micro job: Surveys, rewards program
Pays by: Check on a monthly basis
Participants earn a few cents for each search performed or more by watching ads, taking surveys, shopping online redeeming coupons, receiving emails and playing games. Caution: Inactive accounts' payments may be forfeited and company charges a $3 payout fee.

**InstantBucks** (http://www.instantbucks.com/)
Type of micro job: Surveys, rewards program
Pays in: "Virtual bucks" redeemable for gift cards

**Ipinions** (http://ipinionrewards.com/)

Type of micro job: Surveys on mobile phone
Pays in: Reward points, which can be redeemed for cash in a PayPal account at 100 reward points to one dollar; minimum to redeem is of 500 rewards points. Download the free app; fill out the profile with information such as such as your name, address, gender, and birthday and employment status. You will then be contacted by email, push notifications or phone to participate in surveys that match your profile.

**Microworkers** (http://microworkers.com/)

Type of micro job: Online tasks
Pays with: Money bookers or Alertpay; must have earned $9 to make a withdraw Micro workers put the "micro" in micro jobs. These jobs typically pay a few cents each.

**Mylikes** (http://mylikes.com/)
Type of micro job: Social media advertising
Pays in: Cash in PayPal or Amazon gift cards

**Playgroups USA**
(http://www.flexjobs.com/jobs/telecommuting-jobs-at-playgroups_usa)

Playgroups USA was started by parents that saw the irreplaceable benefits of playgroup years ago and wanted to bring these opportunities to everyone wishing the best for their children. By providing resources and intuitive site tools, visitors can search every US zip code for a playgroup nearby or create their own. Playgroups USA also has an event division called WeeBoogie. WeeBoogie events inspire parents by encouraging music and dance early in a child's life while also supporting local nonprofits that serve young families. Playgroups USA have home based event and account manager opportunities in many major cities around the US as well as remote volunteer opportunities.

**QuickTate** (http://typists.quicktate.com/transcribers/signup)
Type of micro job: Crowd sourcing, transcription
Pays: $.0025 per word or 4 words for 1 cent

**Redlr** (http://pin.redlr.com/signup)
Type of micro job: Online services marketplace, online tasks
Pays in: USD via PayPal or Payza; withdraws may incur PayPal fees

**Reward TV**
(http://www.rewardtv.com/welcome/sampleGames.sdo)
Play trivia for cash and prizes
Watch your favorite
TV shows then visit RewardTV the next day!
Win cash & prizes like gift cards and electronics in our Auctions, Shopping Sprees, and Sweepstakes! You'll earn an entry into our $10,000 Sweepstakes each day you play TV Trivia!

**Scribie** (http://scribie.com/jobs)
Type of micro job: Crowd sourcing, transcription, transcription review and proofreading
Pays: $1 per 6-minute audio segment via PayPal

**Shopkick** (http://www.shopkick.com/)
Type of micro job: Rewards program, online and real-world tasks via mobile phone.
Pays in: Points redeemable for discounts and coupons

**Short task** (http://www.shorttask.com/)
*Short Task* connects online job seekers with providers. Workers can work at home and make money from thousands of tasks and jobs.

**Skyword** (http://www.skyword.com/writers/)
Type of micro job: Writing
Pays in: PayPal account twice a month
Articles earn around $10 plus very small amount for traffic. These micro jobs for writers are probably best for beginners because of the pay scale.

**SwagBucks** (http://www.swagbucks.com/)
Type of micro job: Rewards program
Pays in: "Virtual currency" redeemable for gift cards, coupons, etc.
Users earn SwagBucks by playing games, doing surveys and shopping.

# USERABILITY TESTING

**userfeel.com**
(http://www.userfeel.com/index.php?option=com_content&view=article&id=9&Itemid=23&lang=en&hide=1&utm_expid=32266794-0.QdRzIADkRruvRlxpPKPF_w.1)

He or she conducts a usability test on a site to reveal usability problems on the client's sites.

A good Tester can provide useful information on a site's usability. In a few words:

- Speak her thoughts on the microphone.
- Tell us what confuses him, and what attracts his attention.
- Explain what and why she does what she does on the site.
- Propose something that would help him perform the required task.
- Provide useful comments.
- Perform the required tasks according to the test scenario.
- Speak loudly and clearly on the microphone.
- Thoroughly answer the questions in writing, at the end of the test.

For each test you conduct after the initial sample test, you get paid $10 at the end of each week, via PayPal. The amount of money you can earn depends on how well you speak your thoughts into the microphone, and how useful your usability remarks can be. Also, the amount of tests you get assigned depends on the amount of orders we have. For each test you perform, you get rated by the site's owner. Your overall rating determines the amount of tests you'll be assigned. Anyhow, we don't suggest quitting your regular job, but good testers can earn up to $100-$200 per month.

**StartUpLift** (http://startuplift.com/get-paid-to-provide-feedback/)
Type of micro job: Remote website tester
Pays in USD in PayPal weekly

Testers are paid $10 to spend 10-20 minutes on a website using a screen and voice recorder and giving feedback. Mobile tests pay $15. Jobs are made available based on the demographics of the tester.

**Userlytics** (http:www.userlytics.com/tester)
Userlytics is a highly recognized and respected website usability testing company. Top businesses and well-known websites companies are clients of Userlytics. Seeking the viewpoint of the average online user, Userlytics clients are able to gain a better knowledge of whether they have a user-friendly website. Because clients of Userlytics are interested in the perspective of everyday people, Userlytics allows anyone to become a tester for their clients!

What Do Userlytics Testers Do?
Based on the demographic information provided by Userlytics testers, a variety of assignments may be available. Using Userlytics downloadable program, testers can check the availability of open tests. When one is available, Userlytics testers can choose to start the test. The program window will open the client's website and provide a set of tasks and instructions.
For instance, if such said company, XYZ.com sells alphabet toys, they may be interested in knowing how easy it is for their visitors to find the cost of ABC building blocks. Therefore, the type of tasks may be to search the site for ABC building blocks and locate the price. The Userlytics program records the actions taking place during the test.
Testers are also recorded visually and through audio. It is important for testers to think aloud. Clients of Userlytics want to see and hear the reactions and the thinking process of the testers. Remember, the goal of Userlytics is to project the average online user's experience.

How Does Userlytics Pay?
Userlytics pays through PayPal within two weeks of completing each test. Every test that is completed within the guidelines given pays a generous $10. Each test takes no more than 10 minutes to complete, making the pay well worth the time.

What Are Userlytics Requirements?
Because Userlytics uses both Audio and Visual responses in formatting a user's experience, testers need both a microphone and a webcam. Additionally, a user will need to download Userlytics software, which is quick and easy. Testers with Windows operating system will need to have XP or higher (XP/Vista/7) or Mac users will need Leopard 10.5 or newer. Finally, at least 200 MB of free hard disk space is required. Userlytics looks for people of all demographics and computer experience.

How Can I Sign Up To Be a Tester for Userlytics?
Because Userlytics needs to provide feedback to their clients that include user experience from a range of types of people, anyone who meets the above requirements can work for Userlytics! There is no application approval process, just sign up! Simply visit http://www.userlytics.com/tester/ and register.

**YouEye** (http://join.youeye.com/participant-101/)
Online usability studies are an easy way to earn money from home. You'll be asked to perform simple tasks on a website, such as signing up for an account or adding an item to your shopping cart.

Desktop
You must be 18 years or older and speak English fluently
The current minimum system requirements are **Mac with OS X 10.7** or higher or **PC with Windows Vista, Service Pack II** or higher
You must have access to a webcam and microphone
You must have a fast internet connection - DSL or faster
You must be able to follow instructions

Mobile
You must be 18 years older and speak English fluently
You must have a mobile device with a front facing camera
You must have **iOS 6.1** or higher
You must have **Android 2.3** or higher
You must have Wifi connectivity or cellular connectivity (WiFi preferred)

# COMPUTER TECHNOLOGY AND IT

**The Work Site** (http://www.theworksite.com/)

The worksite offers computer job listings, work from home employment opportunities solutions and employment law information. Find IT Employment Opportunities. We provide an easy to use information technology job search for finding an open position in your field of expertise. Your new, higher paying IT job could be posted on our site. Register for free to begin.

**Snag A Job** (http://www.snagajob.com/job-search/q-part+time+computer+technology)
A Part time job board for people trained in computer technology

**Indeed.com**
(http://www.indeed.com/jobs?q=Work+From+Home+IT&matchtype=b&network=g&device=c&devicemodel=&creative=34027885838&keyword=%2Bwork%20%2Bfrom%20%2Bhome%20%2Bit%20%2Bjobs&place

ment=&param1=&param2=&random=1586959625100396360&aceid=&adposition=1t1&gclid=CITb3On60LsCFYlDMgodzAYASA)
Job board for work at home computer technologists

**Flex Jobs**
(http://www.flexjobs.com/jobs/computer-it)
Part time and some work at home computer technology jobs

**Monster.com**
(http://jobs.monster.com/v-part-time-q-computer-work-from-home-jobs.aspx)
Part time work at home computer technology job positions.

**Outline Systems**
(http://www.flexjobs.com/jobs/telecommuting-jobs-at-outline_systems)

Since 1997, Outline Systems has been providing IT and consulting services to its clients in the insurance industry. The management team at Outline Systems has years of experience in multiple areas with the ability to meet the business needs of each client. The services offered by Outline Systems consist of application development, application maintenance, testing, professional services, infrastructure management, and ITIL process consulting. Outline Systems has developed several web-based products that add overall value for their clients as well as business partnerships with well-known companies such as IBM, Microsoft, Oracle, Cisco, and Sun Microsystems. Outline Systems is a growing company that has been recognized by Inc., Deloitte, CRN, and Software Magazine for their growth. With this continued growth Outline Systems is continually looking for qualified professionals to join their team.


**Lunarpages**
(http://www.lunarpages.com/information/employment/junior-system-administrator-I)

We are looking for people who want a career in systems administration. Varying shifts. Remote positions available.

Description:

- Monitors servers including booting a machine when necessary
- Responds to server alerts as per instructions from supervisory staff
- Responsible for server stability
- Provides technical support for Level I escalation issues via helpdesk, chat, telephone and forums
- Assists Customer Service Representatives with technical support issues

- Transfers accounts between servers when necessary for load balancing or account upgrades
- Continues development of Lunarpages and systems knowledge to more effectively answer calls
- Performs miscellaneous job-related duties as assigned

Skills:

- Knowledge and understanding of operating principles, practices, and procedures within area of business specialty
- Knowledge of Linux required
- Previous server administration a plus
- Knowledge of relational databases including a database query language
- Understanding of PHP and HTML
- Understanding of ASP helpful
- Understanding of JSP helpful
- Ability to communicate effectively, both orally and written
- Ability to work well with the public
- Ability to troubleshoot and resolve customer and server issues
- Skilled in the use of personal computers and related software applications
- Ability to work productively and efficiently to meet deadlines and quotas
- Attention to detail
- Analytical skills
- Ability to work in a team environment
- Knowledge of customer service principles, techniques, systems, and standards

# SOCIAL MEDIA

**Mylikes** (http://mylikes.com/publishers/overview)
Earn money by creating a social website OR embed our sponsored widget on your site to increase revenue and engagement

**Shutter Stock** (http://submit.shutterstock.com/?language=en)
Submit photos and sell them

**SociBuzz** (http://www.socibuzz.com/)
Get started today by promoting the products, services, and causes that match the "voice" of your social media accounts. With SociBuzz, advertisers will pay you for each visitor you send to their websites.

**Pin Booster** (https://pinbooster.com/site/page/view/pinners)
1. Sign up and set your price per pin
We'll give you an idea of a reasonable amount to charge, based on other pinners, but we leave the final price up to you. At Pin booster, you might notice a trend that you're always in the driver's seat.

2. Select the boards you pin in more often
Always pinning home décor? Tell us! This kind of information helps us find the right advertising fit for you. We want your Pin booster pins to be at home with all of your other favorite things.

3. When you receive an offer, decide to accept it or reject it
You'll receive a notification that someone thinks you're awesome and wants to pay you to pin, but then it's up to you whether you want to pin the image or not. Again, you're the boss!

4. If you accept it, pin away!
Love the pin? Accept the offer and get started. We'll walk you through the specifics to make sure that everything goes well, but it's pretty straightforward.

5. Get paid (the good part) within 24 hours of the pin going live
You did your part, now it's time for us to do ours. You should see funds show up in your Pin booster account within 24 hours. Feel free to spend that time scouring Pinterest for ways to spend it.

# JOBS FOR TEENS/COLLEGE STUDENTS
(http://www.onlinejobsteenagers.com/)

If you are of the opinion that looking for an online job for teenagers will involve a long, boring process of interviews, then let me tell you – that's just not the case. As a matter \ of fact, it is quite simple for teenagers to find online jobs and get started with earning money.
Unlike the offline jobs, there is no need for any paper work making it rather convenient for teenager to work online.
Most online jobs can be very educating too while being interesting. These jobs offer flexible work schedules without too much stress on deadlines and targets. This makes it convenient for teenagers like you to balance your work, study and entertainment as per your convenience.

(http://www.today-job.com/online-jobs-for-teenagers)

**Fiverr.com** - Some of the articles you might come across about online jobs for teenagers suggest joining a freelance site like Odesk or Elance and looking for writing jobs or other freelance work. The problem with that though (and something that is often not mentioned in those articles) is that those sites require that everyone who works on the site is over the age of 18. There is no faking it either as you are required to provide the proper proof!

Fiverr.com however is a little different. Fiverr is open to everybody and you can offer a 'gig' for $5 to anyone. The fun thing about Fiverr.com for teenagers is the 'gig' they offer can be anything and sometimes the most unusual ones turn out to be the most popular.
You can offer to do video impersonations, create artwork, take zany pictures; pretend to be someone's girlfriend or boyfriend on Facebook (believe it or not that's a very popular gig!) In fact almost anything goes, as long as it is not illegal or pornographic.

**YouTube** – Making money from the advertising revenue that YouTube videos can earn is another way that teenagers can use their own personal creativity to make money online. As anyone who goes on You Tube knows almost anything and everything has the potential to go viral and a lot of teens have already made plenty of cash, and a name for themselves, with their videos. These days anyone can opt to 'monetize' their videos and then it's just up to you to promote, promote, promote!

**Paid to Click Sites** – Another moneymaking venture that is often suggested for teenagers is that they join a paid survey site. Again though, the vast majority of these sites are for people aged 18 or over. Again, maybe you could fake it but expect trouble when it comes to withdrawing earnings if you do. What a younger teen can consider is joining a pay to click site. Basically you sign up for an account and then are presented with a series of websites that you literally have to click through. It is not always that interesting and the money you earn is not a great deal but if you get into the habit of visiting a site regularly you can earn some extra pocket money.

**Etsy** - Lots of teenagers, even in the age of the Internet, like to make things. Jewelry, buttons, artwork, all kinds of things. Etsy is an online marketplace for all of these things and more. If you are under 18 you will have to have an adult set up a 'store' for you but once they do it's all yours to run. Etsy provides you with a lot of cool tools to help you build a great online storefront and all you will need is a PayPal.

**Start a Blog** - Of all the ways that a teen can make money online blogging is the one that will take the longest to become profitable and it will also probably require the most work. However if you really, really know what you are writing about and can then write about in the long run all the effort can be worth it.

These are just a few ways the Internet can open up earning opportunities for teens.

The one thing you do need to be on the lookout for is scams. Unfortunately there are people out there who try to take advantage of a teen's desire to earn their own money and rip them off. Don't pay to join a site that promises to find you a job.

Anything they could offer you (which is usually nothing at all) you can find for yourself.

If you are a video game fan a site like gameplaysurveys.com should be a good fit for you.

This is one of few online jobs for teenagers you will find pretty straight forward.
With this opportunity you will find that there are many people in the online community which require your fresh and accurate grammar skills to fulfill a project.
Writing articles pays pretty well on a consistent basis.
You will need a computer, internet access, a subscription to one of the many free websites that offer this opportunity, and most of the time a PayPal account were you can get paid. The amount of money you can make here depends on your writing skills, motivation, knowledge on a particular field, and TIME you devote to writing.

***College students are invited to do Micro Tasks for some cash while going to College***

# DIRECTIONS FOR GETTING A PAYPAL ACCOUNT

Start with going to this website:
(https://www/paypal.com/webapps/setup-paypal-account/onboarding/execution=els1)

**Register for personal account**

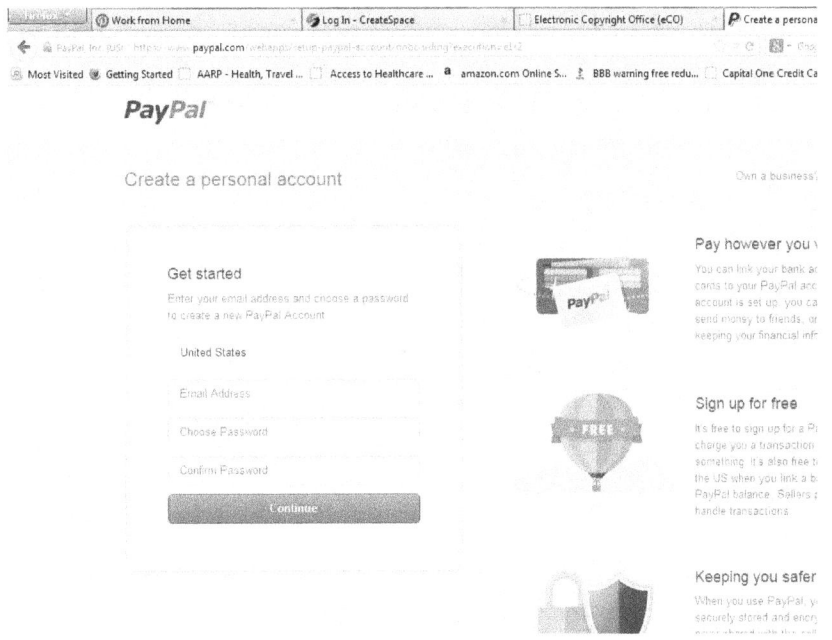

Type in your email address
(This email address will be your login to PayPal)

Create your password then Continue

Next, complete your personal profile information (date of birth, the last 4 digits of social security number)
Review the Terms and Conditions and then "Agree and Continue"

Type in your email address (this email address will be your login to PayPal)
Create your password
Continue

Next, complete your personal profile information (date of birth, the last 4 digits of social security number)
Review the Terms and Conditions and then "Agree and Continue"

Then you will need to complete the PayPal Account set up:
Confirm PayPal Mobile
Confirm email address
Add your bank account

Set up your security questions

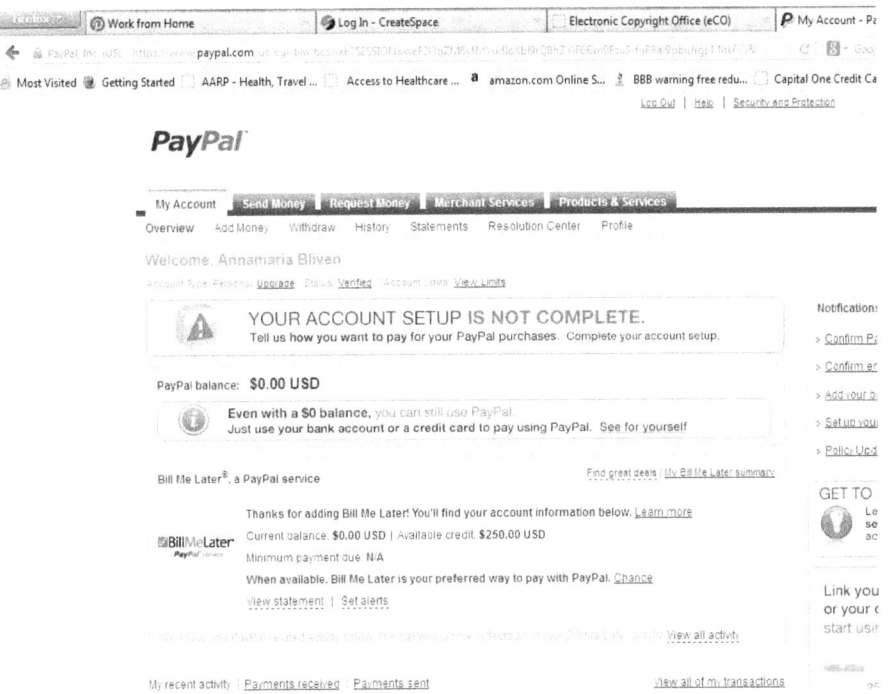

Confirming PayPal mobile is done with a text message or phone call from PayPal

Confirm your email address (with an email that is sent to you from PayPal)

When you add your bank account, you will need the routing number and account number and will be asked to confirm your bank account with two deposits under $1 within a few business days.

Setting up security questions is self-explanatory.

At this point, you are ready to receive payment from doing online work.

# WRAP UP AND DISCLAIMER

According to (http://scottberkun.com/2013/how-many-people-really-work-from-home-research-Summary/) 2.9 million people consider home as their primary place of work. That is 2.3% of today's workforce (and I am one of them—and have been for quite some time!)
**Now it's your turn!**

Regular telecommuting grew by 61% between 2005 and 2009. During that same time period, Home-based self-employment grew by 1.7%.

Based on current trends, with no growth acceleration, regular telecommuters will total 4.9 million.
By 2016, a 69% increase from the current level … so this means that working online from home or any place you choose is a definite possibility.

Most of the information for this book came from the website:
http://workathomemoms.about.com/od/workathomecareers/ss/wahjobdirectory.htm

I included pertinent information about each company and made sure to list the website for you to get more details and register for the jobs. I cannot guarantee that all the websites and jobs listed in the book will be available --- things in the business world are always changing. Please read each job listing carefully ---there may be locality restrictions and you may need to be living in a specific area to qualify for the job. Not all telecommute/remote jobs are like that, only some of them.

I do not guarantee you will be hired but if you follow these tips, you are likely to get hired and keep your job:
1. Be positive ("it takes work to get work") and that is not any different when looking for an online job.
2. Make sure to apply for only the jobs you have experience, skills and ability.
3. Make sure to submit all the paperwork required to be hired in a timely manner.
4. You may have to take an assessment test and go through some training before you are fully hired.
5. Be sure to perform your tasks with excellence.
6. Be sure to cultivate healthy working relationships with your supervisors and co-workers.
Keep in mind that even though you are not sharing an office space, you are sharing a "virtual" working environment.
7. Work with diligence and integrity ---it will definitely pay you dividends!

Some of the companies in the book are listed more than once. This is due to the fact that the companies employ online workers in different capacities.

Here are some other websites you may want to bookmark and **monitor for additional telecommute/remote jobs** as they become available:

www.workersonboard.com

http://www.nextjobathome.net

http://jobs.monster.com/v-part-time-q-work-online-from-home-jobs.aspx

http://www.wahm.com/

http://www.moneymakingmommy.com/

http://www.makemoneyfromonlinejobs.com/

http://www.allyou.com/budget-home/money- shopping/online-jobs-work-from-home-00411000073600/

http://www.onlinejobsteenagers.com/

http://jobsearch.about.com/od/workfromhome/tp/work-at-home.htm

http://voices.yahoo.com/huge-list-paid-online-jury-opportunities-8066268.html?cat=3

http://www.spi-global.com/jobs/career-opportunities-in-madison

http://workathomemoms.about.com/od/workathomecareers/ss/wahjobdirectory.htm

http://realwaystoearnmoneyonline.com

https://www.elance.com/r/jobs/

I invite you to research on your own to find more job opportunities you can work from home and at home.

**\*\*\*IF YOU NEED IMMEDIATE CASH, OR YOU HAVE A CRIMINAL BACKGROUND OR CANNOT PASS A CREDIT CHECK --- IT IS HIGHLY RECOMMENDED YOU DO MICRO TASKS\*\*\*THEY PAY INSTANTLY\*\*\***

www.ingramcontent.com/pod-product-compliance
Lightning Source LLC
Chambersburg PA
CBHW081725170526
45167CB00009B/3704